H-o

CW00504934

DELIRIUM

Created by theatre O
Written by Enda Walsh

first performed on 9th April 2008

a co-production with Barbican (London) and the Abbey Theatre (Dublin)

theatre O

LD 39507483

THEATRE O

theatre O has been creating original work on an international platform since 2000. Under the joint artistic direction of Joseph Alford and Carolina Valdés their previous shows — 3 DARK TALES, THE ARGUMENT and ASTRONAUT — have been seen all around the world to public and critical acclaim. theatre O draws its energy from the outstanding international artists it brings together in a uniquely collaborative way. The combination of these skills and personalities is the basis for creating remarkable and inspirational theatre. *Delirium* is a brand new piece of work made with artists from across England, Ireland, Spain and Australia.

ENDA WALSH

Enda Walsh is a leading contemporary playwright. His previous projects include DISCO PIGS and CHATROOM. He recently won rave reviews and Fringe First Awards at the Edinburgh Festival Fringe for THE WALWORTH FARCE (2007) and THE NEW ELECTRIC BALLROOM (2008). Enda and theatre O have been working together, and establishing collaborative approaches to making theatre, since 2005. DELIRIUM is the first production to come out of this maturing relationship.

THANKS

theatre O and Enda Walsh would like to thank the following people, without whom this project would not have been possible: the families of all the company for their incredible support throughout, Brian Brady and everyone at Laban, David Micklem, Edward Parry, Emma Stenning and Nick Williams, Fiach MacConghail and all at the Abbey Theatre, Gordon Millar, Malin Forbes, Griselda Yorke, Dr. Helen Freshwater, Lil and Aurélien, Louis Chang, Thomas Hicks and Lauren McCalmont, Louise Jeffreys and ~~everyone at BITE, Anne David, Paul Mc11fe, Feter~~ Freeman, Richard ~~~~ Morris and extra special t~~~~

This prod~~~~ Arts Council Engl~~~~ the Alfor~~~~ Trust,

DELIRIUM

Created by THEATRE O
Written by ENDA WALSH
Directed by JOSEPH ALFORD

CAST

Alyosha	JOSEPH ALFORD
Fyodor	DENIS QUILLIGAN
Grushenka	JULIE BOWER
Ivan	DOMINIC BURDESS
Katerina	CAROLINA VALDÉS
Mitya	NICK LEE
Smerdyakov	LUCIEN MACDOUGALL

COLLABORATORS

Animation and Illustration	PADDY MOLLOY
Assistant Director	KATE WASSERBERG
Choreography	EVA VILAMITJANA
Composer and Sound	GUS MACMILLAN
Design	JAMES HUMPHREY
Lighting	AIDEEN MALONE

PRODUCTION TEAM

Company Manager	ROSIE KELLY
Producer	SIMON ZIMMERMAN
Production Manager	ESTELLE RICKELTON
	SIMON BOURNE
Stage Manager	EMMA MCKIE
Stage Manager for the Abbey	STEPHEN DEMPSEY
Technical Manager	NATHAN JOHNSON
Original devisors (not in tonight's company)	CLIVE MENDUS

IF THERE IS NO GOD, EVERYTHING IS PERMITTED.

Celebrated as a literary masterpiece, Dostoevsky's final novel is a story of love and betrayal between a brutal father and his neglected sons: THE BROTHERS KARAMAZOV. DELIRIUM is a daring new theatrical adaptation of this dark and violent work presented by theatre O and multi-award-winning writer Enda Walsh.

Similar to the masterpiece it is based on, DELIRIUM explores a world without morals, depicting the human condition in a harsh and uncompromising way. The determined brothers of the title, and their despicable father, are each driven by an individual mix of passion, intellect, faith and frustration. Feuds over women and money ensue and bad blood runs deep, as beliefs and spitefulness ignite a frenzy of emotion so strong it is impossible to contain. From its explosive opening, this bold and muscular interpretation demands its audiences to sit up and take notice.

'THE BROTHERS KARAMAZOV is a haunting and epic story that deals with the human condition in the most profound way. It is a 'classic' text, but the story is absolutely relevant today, and working with Enda Walsh we have created a powerful and explosive adaptation for a modern audience. We hope you enjoy the piece, and look forward to hearing your thoughts.'

Joseph Alford and Carolina Valdés
Co-Artistic Directors, theatre O

CAST

JOSEPH ALFORD (Alyosha)
is founder and Co-Artistic Director of
theatre O. He is a freelance director and
performer who trained with Jacques Lecoq
in Paris. Theatre credits include: HOW
MUCH IS YOUR IRON? (Young Vic); THE
ARGUMENT, THE LESSON, 3 DARK TALES
(theatre O). Directing credits include:
ERISMENA (English Touring Opera); ARSENIC
AND OLD LACE (Derby Playhouse);
ASTRONAUT, THE ARGUMENT, THE LESSON,
3 DARK TALES (theatre O); TIME AND SPACE
(Beijing Living Dance Studio).

JULIE BOWER (Grushenka)
comes from Wolverhampton in the West
Midlands. In 2000 she went to Oxford
University to read for her degree in
Russian and English literature. During her
degree she undertook a special Author
Study of Dostoevsky and lived in the
Russian Federation for nine months,
working as a researcher and journalist.
She spent a year in New York after taking
her degree and then went to Paris where
she completed the two-year theatre
course at the Jacques Lecoq school.
DELIRIUM is her first major theatre credit.

DOMINIC BURDESS (Ivan)
is a freelance performer and director who
trained with Jacques Lecoq in Paris.
Theatre credits include: PINOCCHIO
(Theatre Royal, Northampton); VOLPONE
(Manchester Royal Exchange); ARSENIC AND
OLD LACE (Derby Playhouse); CHARLIE
CHAPLIN (Proteus); SIGNALS OF DISTRESS
(The Flying Machine, Soho Rep NYC). TV
credits include: Dead Ringers, My Dad's the
PM (BBC). Other recent projects include
directing AFTER MIKUYU (Oval House); and
work with the Verbatim Symposium 2006,
Jamworks, Company F.Z, and Cirque du
Soleil. With his own company, Dominic
created the Total Theatre Award-winning
THE ILLUSION BROTHERS; SOMEBODY TO
LOVE, which toured internationally, and
was filmed and released on DVD by EMI;
and wrote and directed the film THE
MOURNERS, which won Best Screenplay at
the San Francisco Short Film Festival. He
also teaches movement at GSA
Conservatoire, Mountview, Arts Ed. and the
Birmingham School of Acting.

NICK LEE (Mitya)
graduated from the actor-training
programme at Trinity College Dublin in
2003. Theatre credits include: Shawn
Keogh in THE PLAYBOY OF THE WESTERN
WORLD (Druid/Tokyo International Arts
Festival/Perth International Arts Festival,
Australia); THE EMPRESS OF INDIA, THE
YEAR OF THE HIKER (Druid); DRUIDSYNGE –
THE COMPLETE WORKS OF JM SYNGE
(Galway, Dublin, Edinburgh, Inis Meain,
Guthrie Theater Minneapolis & Lincoln
Center Festival in New York City); Michael
Hegarty in THE FREEDOM OF THE CITY
(Finborough Theatre, London); THE
LEGEND OF DEVLIN CASSIDY/MOONLIGHT
MICKEY'S (Calipo Theatre and Picture
Co.); Patrick Kavanagh in THE GREEN
FOOL (Upstate Theatre Project); THE
ILLUSON (Randolf SD/Project Arts Centre,
Dublin). TV and film credits include:
Padraig in SINGLE HANDED – THE STOLEN
CHILD (RTÉ/Touchpaper TV); Michael
Collins in FRONGOCH – UNIVERSITY OF
REVOLUTION (TG4/S4C); James Lester in
the final series of BACHELORS WALK (RTÉ).

LUCIEN MACDOUGALL (Smerdyakov)
is a freelance performer who studied at
Guildford School of Acting, and with
Jacques Lecoq in Paris. Theatre credits
include: an original adaptation of Gogol's
THE NOSE, FLYDRAGON
(Stampede/Gogolia); BOND, 3 DARK TALES
(theatre O); CARMEN, THE BARBER OF
SEVILLE (Opera 21); ARSENIC AND OLD
LACE, ANIMAL FARM, ARABIAN NIGHTS
(Derby Playhouse); PINOCCHIO
(Northampton Royal). Lucien wrote and
performed in ALL MAPPED OUT (Gogolia), a
company for whom he is Artistic Director.
TV credits include: HANNAH GLASSE,
DOMESTIC GODDESS. Short films include:
DROUGHT, and ME MY SWAMI AND I.

DENIS QUILLIGAN (Fyodor)
is a freelance performer whose theatre
credits include: Joxer in JUNO AND THE
PAYCOCK, Father Jack in DANCING AT
LUGHNASA (Edinburgh Lyceum); Canon
Mick O'Byrne in PHILADELPHIA HERE I
COME (The Gaiety Dublin & Liverpool
Playhouse); Steven in POOR BEAST IN THE
RAIN/WEXFORD TRILOGY (The Bush
Theatre); Jimmy in THE PLAYBOY OF THE
WESTERN WORLD (Manchester Royal

Exchange); Scouse Micky in MAY QUEEN (Liverpool Everyman); Dr Burcot in FROBISHER'S GOLD (The Shaw); Hamm in ENDGAME (Bridge Lane); Sir Charles Cameron in FRONGOCH (North Wales Stage); Henry in TRAVELS WITH MY AUNT (Musselburgh); Wolfe Tone in LIFE OF WOLFE TONE (Riverside Studios); Poges in PURPLE DUST (New York Public Theatre). TV and film credits include: King's Surgeon in THE TUDORS, HH Asquith PM in THE MAN WHO LOST IRELAND, Father John McManus in THE BABY WAR, Mr O'Rourke in FATHER TED, Rev. John Beresford in CONSPIRACY OF SILENCE, Billy Reilly in THE BILL.

CAROLINA VALDÉS (Katerina) is Co-Artistic Director of theatre O, and a freelance director and performer who trained with Jacques Lecoq in Paris. Carolina's theatre credits include: CASSANOVA (Told By An Idiot); LYNDIE'S GOT A GUN (Paines Plough); ASTRONAUT, THE ARGUMENT, THE LESSON, 3 DARK TALES (theatre O). Theatre directing includes: ALL MAPPED OUT (Gogolia); THE BARBER OF SEVILLE (Carmen, Opera 21); THE GARDEN (Shams). Movement director on ABSURDIA (Donmar Warehouse).

CREATIVE TEAM

NATHAN JOHNSON (Technical Manager) has been a London-based freelance technical stage manager for three years and before that worked in education and live events. Before joining theatre O, Nathan had been touring with Theatre-Rites and Russell Maliphant Dance Company around the UK and Europe as a re-lighter and sound number one, as well as working on shows in the West End such as BAD GIRLS THE MUSICAL, JAY JOHNSON, THE TWO AND ONLY and TREATS. As a sound engineer Nathan has worked with artists such as: Radiohead, Hard-Fi, The Kooks, James Brown and Billy Bragg.

GUS MACMILLAN (Composer and Sound) has worked in the arts industry over the last eighteen years as a composer, musician and sound designer. Based in Melbourne, Australia, he spent most of the 90s performing as a multi-instrumentalist with Blue Grassy Knoll, and conceived, co-wrote and produced live scores to the silent films of Buster Keaton. These shows received five-star reviews at the 1999 and 2000 Edinburgh Festival and have toured internationally ever since. In 2004 he completed a Graduate Diploma Course in Sound Design at Victorian College of the Arts, working with sound and music in a variety of different of art forms, including dance, theatre, film, documentary, circus and puppetry. He is composer-in-residence for Red Span Dance Company. He has his own recording studio and continues to write, perform, and teach music. Gus was also the 2005 Guildford Banjo Jamboree's two-tune pick-off champion.

EMMA MCKIE (Stage Manager) trained at the Royal Scottish Academy of Music and Drama. Company Management credits include: FORGOTTEN PEACOCK (Artluxe); TWELFTH NIGHT (Sprite Productions). Stage Management credits include: DIDO AND AENEAS (Armonico Consort); I CAUGHT CRABS IN WALBERSWICK, SWITZERLAND (HighTide 2008); COSI FAN TUTI, 8000M, RINALDO (RSAMD); EUGENE ONEGIN (RSAMD/Scottish Opera); HAMLET (Citizens' Theatre); IRON CURTAIN, THE CONFESSIONS OF JULIAN PO (Edinburgh Fringe Festival 2007).

AIDEEN MALONE (Lighting Designer) trained in Dublin and London. She has worked extensively in theatre, dance and opera since 1994. Some of the companies she has collaborated with are: English Touring Opera, Theatre Rites, Clod Ensemble, Akram Khan Company, Angika Dance Company, The Bush Theatre and Paco Pena. Her future projects with Angika Dance Company and Shobana Jeyasingh.

PADDY MOLLOY (Illustrator and Animator) trained in Illustration and Animation at Kingston University, graduating in 2004. Working from his studio in London, Paddy is a regular contributor to the GUARDIAN (UK) and the GLOBE AND MAIL (Canada); as well as producing bespoke work for clients, including BIG ISSUE, TIME OUT, RADIO TIMES, BUSINESS WEEK (US); ESTATES GAZETTE and Random House.

ESTELLE RICKELTON (Production Manager) studied Drama and Theatre Arts at Goldsmiths College, London, where she specialised in Lighting Design. She worked at the Robin Howard Theatre in London as a full time Theatre Technician before beginning work with Russell

Maliphant Dance Company as Sound Engineer in 2002, subsequently taking over as Technical Manager and then Production Manager. Estelle has toured with several other dance and theatre companies including: Clod Ensemble, EDge Dance Company, BGroup and Akram Khan Company, where she was sound engineer for part of the tour of KAASH and RONIN, and technical manager for the classical programme, Third Catalogue. Estelle has lit many productions, collaborating with Stephanie Schober, Anton Lachky and Eulalia Ayguade, Sorted Productions, Minicab Productions and Akademi.

EVA VILAMITJANA (Choreographer) trained as a contemporary dancer and choreographer at Institut del Teatre, Barcelona, and completed her studies at New York, North Carolina, Paris and Wien. She has won awards at the International Tanzwochen (Wien); the American Dance Festival (North Carolina); the Certamen Coreográfico (Madrid); and the Premio Ricard Moragas (Barcelona). As a performer she has toured throughout Europe and North and South America with Joe Alegado, Bebeto Cidra, Mar Gómez, Trànsit, Pepe Hevia, Las Malqueridas, Nats Nus Nens, El Liceu (Barcelona); theatre O (UK, with whom she has also worked as an actress), and Buissionère (Switzerland). As a choreographer, her credits include: 3 DARK TALES, THE ARGUMENT, ASTRONAUT (theatre O); COMÉDIE MUSICAL VOYAGE (France); ENTRE TRES'S LAXIS RE, DESMAI, QUASI PESA and the OPERAS L'ELISIR D'AMORE (G.Donizetti); RULETA, OPERA PARA UN FIN DE SIGLO. Eva is co-founder of Entre Tres Dance Company (Barcelona).

ENDA WALSH (Writer) is one of Ireland's most widely performed contemporary playwrights. An award-winning writer for theatre and film, his feature film HUNGER won the Camera d'Or for Best New Feature at the Cannes Film Festival 2008. Theatre credits include: THE NEW ELECTRIC BALLROOM (Druid at Galway Arts Festival and Edinburgh Festival Fringe 2008, Fringe First winner; previously at Kammerspeil Theatre, Munich, winner of Theater Heute's Best Foreign Play 2005); THE WALWORTH FARCE (Druid at Galway Arts Festival, Edinburgh Festival Fringe 2007; Dublin, New York and National Theatre,

London, 2008); CHATROOM (National Theatre, London, March 2006 and Autumn 2007); THE SMALL THINGS (Paines Plough, Menier Chocolate Factory, London and Galway Arts Festival 2005); two short plays, HOW THESE MEN TALK (Zurich Shauspielehaus) and LYNDIE'S GOTTA GUN (for Artista Unidos, Lisbon's National Theatre); BEDBOUND (Dublin Theatre Festival 2000; Edinburgh 2001, Fringe First Winner; Royal Court, London; New York and worldwide); MISTERMAN (Granary Theatre); DISCO PIGS (Cork, Dublin 1996; Edinburgh 1997; West End 1998; awarded Arts Council Playwrights Award 1996, Best Fringe Production 1996, and the Stewart Parker and George Devine Awards 1997); THE GINGER ALE BOY (Corcadorca). Film credits include: DISCO PIGS (Temple Films/Renaissance); HUNGER (Blast/FilmFour) winner of the Camera D'Or in this year's Cannes Film Festival and winner of the Sydney Film Festival. Film in development include: CHATROOM (for Ruby Films/FilmFour); ISLAND OF THE AUNTS (an adaptation of Eva Ibbotson's children's novel for Cuba Pictures); KINDERBOY (BBC). Radio credits include: FOUR BIG DAYS IN THE LIFE OF DESSIE BANKS (RTÉ Radio, winner of the PPI Award for Best Radio Drama 2001); THE MONOTONOUS LIFE OF LITTLE MISS P (BBC, commended in the Berlin Prix Europa 2003).

KATE WASSERBERG (Assistant Director) is Associate Director of the Finborough Theatre, London, where her directing credits include: SONS OF YORK, LITTLE MADAM, THE REPRESENTATIVES and I WISH TO DIE SINGING. Other directing includes: SWITZERLAND (Hightide Festival); TEST DRIVE (Soho Theatre Studio); DOING LINES (The Pleasance). Assistant Directing includes: HOLDING FIRE! (Shakespeare's Globe); HOW MUCH IS YOUR IRON? (Young Vic); THE BLUE ROOM (Theatre Royal Bath).

ABBEY THEATRE

The Abbey Theatre is Ireland's national theatre. Since it first opened its doors in 1904, the theatre has played a vital and often controversial role in the literary, social and cultural life of Ireland. The Abbey continues to produce an annual programme of diverse, engaging and innovative Irish and international theatre and to invest in and promote new Irish writers and artists.

Over the years, the Abbey Theatre has contributed some of the world's greatest theatrical works from writers such as J.M. Synge and Sean O'Casey, as well as contemporary classics from the likes of Brian Friel, Frank McGuinness, Tom Murphy and Mark O'Rowe. We are delighted to continue that tradition by presenting new plays by Marina Carr, Tom MacIntyre, Billy Roche and Sam Shepard in our forthcoming season.

Visit www.abbeytheatre.ie for information about our programme of new writing for Autumn 08 — Spring 09.

Board
Bryan McMahon (Chairman), **Catherine Byrne, Tom Hickey, Olwen Fouéré, Suzanne Kelly, Declan Kiberd, Dr Jim Mountjoy, Eugene O'Brien, Maurice O'Connell, Lynne Parker, John Stapleton**

Executive

Fiach Mac Conghail	Director
Declan Cantwell	Director of Finance and Administration
Aideen Howard	Literary Director
Sally Anne Tye	Director of Public Affairs
Tony Wakefield	Director of Technical Services and Operations

Characters

ALYOSHA, *twenty-three*
MITYA, *twenty-seven, Alyosha's brother*
IVAN, *twenty-six, Alyosha's brother*
FYODOR, *fifty-five, their father*
SMERDYAKOV, *twenty-four, their servant*
KATERINA, *twenty-nine, Mitya's fiancée*
GRUSHENKA, *twenty-three, Mitya and Fyodor's lover*
FATHER ZOSIMA, *Alyosha's Elder, a voice*

This text went to press before the end of rehearsals and so may differ slightly from the play as performed.

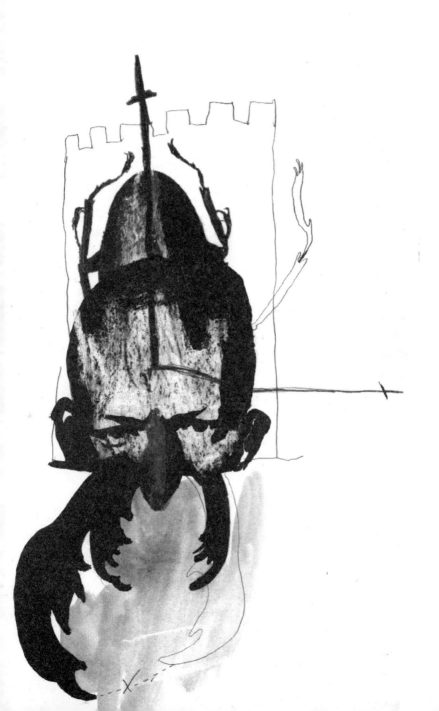

ACT ONE

Scene One

The lights come up on the innocent ALYOSHA, *dressed in a large green poncho. We hear the Northern English voice of his Elder,* FATHER ZOSIMA. ALYOSHA *writes* FATHER ZOSIMA*'s words into a notebook.*

FATHER ZOSIMA. We are all interwoven, us people. We all have a shared responsibility for the sins of the world... so our first action must be to forgive lovingly. If an evil spirit rises up inside you – repeat a prayer to yourself. Do not abandon God and He will not abandon you. Remember always to live your life in faith, to love others unconditionally, to devote your life to goodness... but always to forgive. (*Pause.*) Now, Alyosha... begin with your family. Pray for your father's troubled soul, help your brother Ivan find some peace in himself, some love for his heart. Be with them both in your father's house and wait for Mitya. It is Mitya who will drag a violent future onto all your heads and this is why I'm speaking to you, Alyosha. I saw it in his eyes. A terrible fate shaped from hatred and jealousy. A maddening force that only you can stop, Alyosha. Do not judge your brother... but listen, understand and forgive him. In your sorrow – seek happiness. Work unceasingly for goodness. Be strong. Now be with your family. Love them. (*Slight pause.*) Alyosha?

ALYOSHA *stops writing.*

ALYOSHA. Yes, Father Zosima.

FATHER ZOSIMA. Live.

Scene Two

Impossibly loud music.

MITYA *slams into* ALYOSHA, *knocking him to the floor.*

MITYA *grabs his father,* FYODOR, *and starts to beat him incessantly.*

His brother IVAN *tries to stay out of the way as* ALYOSHA *tries desperately to stop them.*

In the shadows stands the servant SMERDYAKOV. *He films them.*

During the fight IVAN, SMERDYAKOV *and* ALYOSHA *drag the furniture of the living room into place. As well as the dialogue between* MITYA *and* FYODOR, *the others are also shouting to each other and to the brawling men. We listen hard and hear snatches of dialogue.*

MITYA. Grushenka! Grushenka!

FYODOR (*to* SMERDYAKOV). Get me a knife!

SMERDYAKOV *keeps filming.*

Smerdyakov?!

SMERDYAKOV. The knives are in the dishwasher, boss.

During the fight we hear – and, significantly, ALYOSHA *can hear – the voice of* FATHER ZOSIMA.

FATHER ZOSIMA. Everything is an ocean. Everything flows. A small movement, a whisper maybe and that movement is felt on the other side of the world.

The fight continues.

MITYA. With my hands I'll rip you apart, insect!

FYODOR. Hold him!

MITYA. I need to speak with her! (*Calls.*) Grushenka!

FATHER ZOSIMA. So, every day and every moment of that day, walk round yourself. See that your image is a good one, Alyosha.

FYODOR. Out of my house, you thief! You think I'll allow you steal my woman?!

FATHER ZOSIMA. Don't allow the sin of men to confound your work.

MITYA. WHERE?! ARE! YOU! KEEP! ING! HER!

FYODOR. Nowhere!

FATHER ZOSIMA. Don't feel overawed by sin and say that, 'Sin is mighty, we are lonely, wickedness is wearing us away, is killing my good work.'

The fight continues. MITYA *may kill his father.*

MITYA. I know it's tonight! I know it's in Mokroe! Tell me where she's hiding…!

FATHER ZOSIMA. You are working for the whole, for the future. Look for no reward and don't fear those more powerful than you.

At the moment that MITYA *is about to throw his suitcase down onto* FYODOR*'s head, there is a movement from the whole group. The fight ends with a cry of:*

ALYOSHA (*screams*). NO!

Slight pause.

FATHER ZOSIMA. Be wise and serene.

ALYOSHA *only hears white noise. He calls out to* FATHER ZOSIMA.

ALYOSHA. Zosima…?! Father Zosima…?

Scene Three

MITYA *enters the living room with his suitcase. He's late.*

FYODOR. Hasn't he got a good tan, boys? The usual place or was it somewhere new?

MITYA. I'm sorry I'm late, Alyosha.

MITYA *throws* ALYOSHA *a small duty-free bag.*

Little present I bought you. Open in private. Are you well, Ivan?

IVAN. Four months here; I'm imploding.

MITYA. Successful dinner?

IVAN. Not for the turkey.

IVAN *sips his Advocaat.* MITYA *sits.*

Have you seen Katerina yet?

MITYA. Tomorrow maybe.

IVAN. She's missed you.

MITYA. Right.

FYODOR. We all have, haven't we? Would have been nice to eat together.

MITYA. I did apologise.

FYODOR. That's right, you did. First thing you said.

FYODOR *rings the bell for the servant,* SMERDYAKOV.

Brandy!

IVAN. Bring me a yogurt!

SMERDYAKOV *pours* FYODOR *a brandy and then goes to get the yogurt.*

FYODOR. Where was it you was, Mitya? On holiday?

MITYA. Initially?

FYODOR. 'Initially'?!

MITYA. Well, after…

FYODOR. I myself haven't seen the sun in months. Have you holidayed recently, Alyosha? Of course, you visited Rostov Cathedral with Zosima! But that wasn't really a holiday.

IVAN. A holiday for seminarians.

FYODOR. That's work. Did you tan, Aloysha? Of course you didn't tan! You were inside, praying for my sins. We should all be thankful for Aloysha. Each one of us should thank God for such a blessing.

IVAN. That's true.

MITYA. It is true.

They toast and drink.

A long pause and an 'out-of-time' moment for IVAN.

IVAN *stares over at* MITYA. *He stares at his fine clothes, his posture, his superior jaw.*

As he watches him they are isolated by light and we hear what's going on inside IVAN's *head. The sounds of* MITYA *having wild sex with* KATERINA, GRUSHENKA, *just about anyone.*

IVAN *is then aware of his grip on his glass. He's very tense.*
Extremely tense.

His hand suddenly spasms sending the Advocaat splattering
against his jacket.

We are back in the living room again.

IVAN. Balls.

SMERDYAKOV *arrives with a Petits Filous.*

SMERDYAKOV. Your mixed fruit, sir.

IVAN. I'm what?

SMERDYAKOV. Your Petits Filous.

IVAN. Oh.

IVAN *takes it.*

IVAN *scrapes the Advocaat off his jacket with the yogurt spoon.*
He taps it into SMERDYAKOV's *open hand.*

MITYA *sees that* ALYOSHA *looks distant and sad.*

MITYA (*to* ALYOSHA). Are ya okay?

IVAN. He's in mourning.

MITYA. For who…?

IVAN (*whispers*). The priest…

FYODOR. Well, this is nice! All of us here like this. Together. As a
family. As families often do. Evenings just like this one; all too
uncommon for us unfortunately, circumstances having pre-
vented us seeing one another for years… but here we are, our
kindred spirits united once more. Lovely. Makes for an even
happier reunion… the fact that it's been so long.

He goes to ALYOSHA.

Alyosha. The invisible glue which binds us all together! I love
you. Ashamed to say I've used those words too often. But I mean
it this time. I have an idea what God has in store for me. I've
been reckless with life, but I made you and that must count for
something, hey? You are the only true light in my life and 'love'
seems like too small a word suddenly. (*Slight pause.*) Ivan… my

9

crazy genius; these last four months I've had the pleasure of your company. Have enjoyed our discussions. Baffled by his intelligence. His brilliant mind. I'm sure to lose you back to the literati, but while I have you here I'll value each moment.

IVAN (*blank*). Wonderful.

Pause.

FYODOR. And Mitya… well, let's face it… you can always expect your duds, your blacker than black sheeps… but what's not needed is some profligate boy-stallion cavorting around Europe with more spunk than sense…

MITYA. Oh, shut the fuck up!

FYODOR. You shut the fuck up!

IVAN (*triggering the fight*). And go.

FYODOR. You've kept us waiting! What do you expect!

MITYA. I rang to say I'd be late!

FYODOR. You rang me!?

MITYA. I rang from the plane!

FYODOR. You think I wouldn't remember that?!

MITYA. I left a message with what's-his-name.

FYODOR. Smerdyakov, do you have a message for me?

SMERDYAKOV. She called again.

FYODOR. Who called?

SMERDYAKOV. Grushenka.

MITYA. Grushenka called here? What did she say?

SMERDYAKOV. 'I'll take the three grand, Fyodor.'

MITYA. 'I'll take the three grand'!? What does that mean?!

FYODOR. Do you have a message relating to Mitya, blockhead!?

SMERDYAKOV. He'll be late, he rang from the plane.

FYODOR. Where was it you was on holiday?!

MITYA. Why do you need to know?!

10

FYODOR. I want to know where my money is being spent! At least afford me the decency of telling me where you're pissing my money up the wall!

MITYA. The money isn't yours! It's mine from my mother. To see your name fall into my bank account... when I think of what she meant to you! It sickens me!

FYODOR. Can't imagine you care about your dead mother all that much. What are you doing here?

MITYA. I came for dinner.

FYODOR. You missed fucking dinner.

MITYA. My intention was to come for dinner and then perhaps have a discussion...!

FYODOR. Smerdyakov, do we have any more turkey!?

SMERDYAKOV. Might be able to scrape some off the arse.

FYODOR. Then stop whatever you're doing and fix Mitya a cold plate! We need to have a discussion!! What are you doing here?

MITYA. Visiting.

FYODOR. Is it money-related visiting?

MITYA. Partly.

FYODOR. You've come of age and you want the rest?

MITYA. I calculated three thousand!

FYODOR. Oh, you 'calculated' three thousand. I've heard the gossip right, then! You stole three grand, you bad boy!

MITYA (*thrown*). Who told you that...?!

IVAN *clears his throat.*

FYODOR. Well, there's none left! You've spent it all. There's nothing!

MITYA. Don't I have land?! Some woods! I remember reading something about fifty acres...

FYODOR. Oh, that was settled a long time ago! It's sold! Not only have you pissed my money up the wall, you've laid the foundations for that wall, you built the wall, then you pissed it up the wall. Then you get off a plane from Corfu or wherever the fuck you've been, you hire yourself a Hummer H3 and arrive here four hours late with your perma-tan and beg for even more money! The pot is empty! Fuck off!

MITYA. This is about Grushenka.

FYODOR. Is it about Grushenka?

MITYA. What are you paying her three grand for?!

FYODOR. Oh, this and that!

MITYA (*desperate*). But we are in love!

FYODOR. Are we in love, Mitya?!

MITYA. Grushenka and I are in love! AND IF YOU DARE INTERFERE WITH HER I WILL TEAR THAT FUCKING HEAD OFF!

FYODOR. Out of my house, you animal!

MITYA. She is mine!

FYODOR. Well, where is she then?! (*Slight pause*.) Don't you know where she is?! You don't know where she is! You may be in love with her, but it's all one way, Mitya! She's hiding from you!

MITYA. What are you doing with her?

FYODOR. A club I bought. Right now just working out the details, but it seems Grushenka's offering her services for the opening night, right, Smerdyakov?

SMERDYAKOV. All yours for three thousand.

FYODOR. Cheap at half the price!

MITYA. Where is this club!?

FYODOR. The 'where' and the 'when' have fuck all to do with you, son.

MITYA. Alyosha, what do you know about this club?! Ivan?! Ivan, speak!

IVAN. I'm not getting involved!

FYODOR. Now let me spell out the situation, Mitya.

MITYA *takes out his mobile phone and tries to phone*
GRUSHENKA.

FYODOR *grabs the bell.*

FYODOR. Grushenka is closer in love with me than with you.
(*Ding!*) You are engaged to Katerina, a woman with more
beauty and class in her little fingernail than you have in that
whole thieving body of yours. (*Ding!*)

MITYA (*to the phone*). ANSWER!

FYODOR. A woman you've betrayed with whores and Gypsies. Yet
still she loves her little thief?! You are engaged to Katerina!
(*Ding!*) Engaged! (*Ding!*) Engaged! (*Ding!*) Engaged! (*Ding!*)
Engaged!

MITYA. COME ON!

FYODOR. You are nothing but a pumped-up ladies' man with
more cock than conscience. Still... you are here and that at least
completes the family. (*Ding!*)

GRUSHENKA *is heard leaving her answering-machine*
message.

GRUSHENKA. It's Grushenka, of course. Leave a message after
my beep. (*Slight pause.*) Beep.

MITYA *screams in anger/anguish. He slumps, devastated.*

SMERDYAKOV *arrives with a sizeable cold plate of turkey for*
MITYA.

SMERDYAKOV. Quite a large arse on that bird. Careful of the
iron pellets.

Blackout.

Scene Four

A light comes up on an anxious ALYOSHA.

ALYOSHA (*trying to find the correct words*). Do not judge your
brother. Pray for your father's soul... for Ivan's heart. But it is
Mitya... A violent future will be brought down... Forgive and...

13

Frustrated that he can't remember the words, he reaches for his notebook. He kneels on the ground and searches through his notebook for guidance.

The book begins to disintegrate in his hands. He panics.

SMERDYAKOV *slowly appears at the edge of the light and watches him for a moment.*

ALYOSHA *frantically tries to put the pages back together.*

As he does this, the other characters bring on the rest of the set, but with their focus on ALYOSHA. *The pressure is on him.*

SMERDYAKOV *walks behind the puppet booth.*

Scene Five

SMERDYAKOV *wheels his screen forward to the sound of a fairground organ. He then tells his version of the marriage of* FYODOR *to Adelaida and the birth of* MITYA. *The show is accompanied throughout by crass sound effects.*

MITYA *stands in the shadows watching.*

SMERDYAKOV. Ladies and gentlemen, I present to yoooou the exceptionally banal and boring tale of Fyodor's first wife, Adelaida and their idiot son, Mitya!!

The FYODOR PUPPET *appears above the screen. Fart. Burp. Spit.*

FYODOR PUPPET. FYODOR! I thank you!

SMERDYAKOV *appears next to the* FYODOR PUPPET.

SMERDYAKOV. All right, boss?

FYODOR PUPPET. All right, bastard, what are you doing here?

SMERDYAKOV. You're the bastard!

FYODOR PUPPET. No, you're the bastard!

SMERDYAKOV. No, you're the bastard!

FYODOR PUPPET. No, you're the fucking bastard!

SMERDYAKOV. Hey, boss… I see you've got a bit of an erection.

14

FYODOR PUPPET. What? Oh yeah.

SMERDYAKOV. You know what you need to do with that...? Put it in a nice bit of crumpet.

The ADELAIDA PUPPET *appears. The* FYODOR PUPPET *zips over and quickly fucks her to the sound of the Bridal March.*

FYODOR PUPPET. I take thee, I take thee, I TAKE THEE!

After fucking her, FYODOR *disappears to the sound of cheering children. The* ADELAIDA PUPPET *starts gasping and groaning and gives birth to* MITYA.

ADELAIDA PUPPET. PUSH, PUSH!

The infant MITYA PUPPET *appears, bawling his eyes out. He's repulsive and bizarre-looking.*

Ohhh, Mitya!

She kisses him.

MITYA PUPPET. Mummy!

ADELAIDA PUPPET. Mitya!

MITYA PUPPET. Mummy!

ADELAIDA PUPPET. Night night, Mitya – go to sleep now.

The MITYA PUPPET *lies down to sleep.*

Oh. What a lovely day!

A KEN *doll appears.*

ADELAIDA PUPPET. Ooooooh!

KEN. You... complete me.

ADELAIDA PUPPET fawns all over KEN.

ADELAIDA PUPPET. Oh, Ken, Ken Ken! Mitya, Mitya. Oh Ken, Ken. No, Mitya. No, Ken, Mitya, Ken, Mitya – Ken, KEN!

The ADELAIDA PUPPET *disappears off with* KEN. *The* MITYA PUPPET *awakens. Yawns. Looks around for his mother.*

MITYA PUPPET. Mummy! Mummy?! Mummy? Mummy? Mummy! MUMMY! MUMMMYYY!

He starts bawling. The FYODOR PUPPET *appears.*

FYODOR PUPPET. FYODOR! I thank you!

MITYA PUPPET. Daddy! Daddy!

FYODOR PUPPET. Uuh? Who the fuck are you?

MITYA PUPPET. Mitya.

FYODOR PUPPET. Mitya? Doesn't ring a bell.

Porn music starts and a naked Barbie doll appears.

Oooh. SexySexy! Oh, Mitya. SexySexy? Mitya? SEXYSEXY!

The FYODOR PUPPET *disappears, fucking the Barbie.*

MITYA PUPPET. Daddy? Mummy? Daddy? Mummy?

He bawls again even louder this time.

SMERDYAKOV. Oh, shut up! Fuck off!

SMERDYAKOV *throws the* MITYA PUPPET *behind the screen. He looks out.*

I thank you.

Sound of applause.

Scene Six

MITYA *and* ALYOSHA *stand in a room in a Travelodge.*

MITYA. Where's the mini-bar?! I need a little confidence for what I'm about to tell you. You have no idea what it's like living with this brain. It's like I've been wired by a blind, evil man who's cracked my skull open and thrown a food mixer inside… with a fox! A normal person would see a pattern to the day. Like a series of tasks and challenges that have to be undertaken, that must be completed. But for me the world lives in Technicolor, it's a Disneyland with the rides replaced by pure emotions. Can you imagine such a place? It's magnificent! And it's SO fucking expensive! I need that three thousand! Can I speak honestly to you? Will you look past the drink? (*Slight pause.*) I really would like to be good. (*Slight pause.*) So this is it, this is why I've called you here, this is the first part of my confession.

He sits.

I love dirty women. I've had a lot of ladies, of course, but I'm always drawn to the back alleys behind the main road, to the precious gems in the shite. I'm speaking figuratively to protect you from the details. But I love vice. I love the indignity of vice. Besides the indignity of vice there are other things I love about the world of vice of which I'm trying very, very, very hard not to speak about to protect your innocence. The things I'm trying very hard not to speak about are the firm naked backsides in the alleyways. The pert nipples that accompany these backsides. The groping... The exchange of bodily fluids... The chafing... The dull grinding... The slap-happy sound of skin against skin. Oh Jesus! Jesus Christ!! (*He adjusts his penis.*) So this is my world, and into this world stepped Katerina. Back then I was a lieutenant in the army. I looked great in the uniform. My colonel, who hated me, had a daughter, Katerina. She was smart, elegant. Cultured people buzzed about her like buzzing, cultured things. Everything she touched glowed. The way that she could turn a phrase. Beautiful details! Once I tried to speak to her, but she looked right through me, Alyosha. I didn't like that. Not long after I discovered that her father owed a lot of money and if he didn't pay it back his family would be fucked. All of a sudden I saw a way to get my own back. I wrote to her. 'If you need the money, come to me in secret; I'm sure we can work something out.' Now, this is the scene. You go out and come back as Katerina. Go! GO!

ALYOSHA *leaves,* KATERINA *enters.*

The following dialogue is recorded, played over the speakers and mimed by the actors.

MITYA (*on the phone*). And what do you mean by that? You think that matters to me? You want me to come over now?

MITYA *watches* KATERINA *and continues on the phone.*

Well, maybe I will come over. Yeah, I can do that. You want me to do it?

He barks and pants.

I'll fuck you whatever way you want. See you in an hour.

KATERINA (*recorded*). You said if I came to you, you'd give my family the money? Give it to me.

She holds out her hand. He remains still.

Give it to me!

KATERINA *takes her hair down, takes off her blouse and walks towards* MITYA. *He pulls her towards him. She unbuttons his shirt and starts to undo his trousers.*

Suddenly he pushes her away.

MITYA (*recorded*). Stop.

He is breathless, nervous.

I'll send the money on. Now go. Go.

KATERINA *kneels and kisses his hand. She turns to leave, but* MITYA *holds onto her and brings her close to him.*

The following speech is spoken live.

What had it taken for her to come to my room and offer what she offered? I stood in that room alone, Alyosha. Scooped out. Ashamed of myself. Hearing more than any other time that Karamazov insect scratching inside my belly. Her father had no sooner paid his debt and he dropped dead, the fat bastard.

She left town, her own fortune changing courtesy of a rich, dead relative. She sends me back the money she owes and a letter with the sweet words:

KATERINA (*recorded*). For what you have done, I love you madly. Even if you don't love me yet, Mitya... it doesn't matter. Be my husband. Don't be afraid. Your Katya. Kiss. Kiss. Kiss.

She kisses him. He swoons. It's love.

She goes and ALYOSHA *returns.*

MITYA (*live*). We're seconds engaged and she handed me three thousand to post to her sick aunt. I'm rushing to the post office... I trip and fall... I look up to see what idiot has gotten in my way and I see this vision...

The beautiful GRUSHENKA *suddenly appears.*

GRUSHENKA (*recorded*). Grushenka.

MITYA (*live*). I took Katya's money and Grushenka and I went to the ballroom in Mokroe. I got Gypsies and vodka and sent those thousands flying! This is the man I am! This is the eternal insect! Fuck it! I need to repay Katerina! I need to break our engagement!

Scene Seven

SMERDYAKOV *stands in the space with his tape recorder. He presses the button and listens to a brief recording from dinner that evening.*

FYODOR (*recorded*). And you've many friends in Moscow?

IVAN (*recorded*). Too many to mention!

FYODOR (*recorded*). And you sit and discuss the eternal questions?

IVAN (*recorded*). The conversation may become populist at times, but the eternal questions take the greater slice of the evening.

FYODOR (*recorded*). It sounds wonderful.

IVAN (*recorded*). We're a wonderful bunch of people!

FYODOR (*recorded*). And you're popular, Ivan?

IVAN (*recorded*). I couldn't be more popular if I had a profiterole as a head. People love me!

FYODOR (*recorded*). And why is that?

IVAN (*recorded*). My masterly and comedic use of apophasis, most likely.

SMERDYAKOV *stops the tape and presses the button once more. The word 'apophasis' is heard repeating again and again in various voices. All* SMERDYAKOV's. *It stops and suddenly we hear* SMERDYAKOV *masturbating. We hear the sound of frightened pigs.*

SMERDYAKOV *listens to the sounds and slowly licks his lips.*

IVAN *appears, sitting in the space, reading a book.*

SMERDYAKOV *approaches behind him.*

IVAN *answers his mobile phone.* SMERDYAKOV *turns off his tape recorder.*

KATERINA *appears, on the phone.*

KATERINA (*sweetly*). Ivan, are you awake?

IVAN. Yes, yes, I am awake. Fully.

KATERINA. I wondered what you were doing in the morning? I need to ask your advice about something very important. Will you come over for breakfast?

IVAN. Of course, yes. Oh, and I... ahh... I have a little something for you. To give.

KATERINA. Lovely. See you at eight.

KATERINA*'s gone.*

IVAN. Bye bye.

IVAN *kisses his phone.*

SMERDYAKOV. It's been very nice to have you around the house these four months.

IVAN *quickly turns around.*

The level of conversation has risen.

IVAN. You could bring a retarded pig into this house and the collective intelligence would double.

IVAN *goes to leave.*

SMERDYAKOV. The word 'apophasis'? You used it at dinner...

IVAN *stops.*

IVAN. What does it mean, you mean?

SMERDYAKOV. Yes, I couldn't find a definition and I wondered...

IVAN *suddenly notices that* SMERDYAKOV*'s holding the tape recorder and microphone.*

IVAN. What are you doing?

SMERDYAKOV. Something for my studies.

IVAN. What studies?

SMERDYAKOV. The books in this house...

IVAN. The books?!

SMERDYAKOV. The collection of autobiographies are not very taxing. I hate them.

SMERDYAKOV *holds out the microphone.*

If you don't mind...

IVAN. Whatever. Pour me a nightcap.

SMERDYAKOV *gets him a brandy.*

'Apophasis'… from the Greek '*apophanai*'… 'to say no'. Telling what something is by telling what it is not. A process of elimination. Affirmation through negation.

SMERDYAKOV. You determine what it is by what it isn't?

IVAN. We're all familiar with the schoolyard guessing game which uses apophatic inquiry and may begin with the words, 'Is it larger than a bratwurst sausage? Is it more muscle than gristle? Is it violently bulbous?' etcetera. But apophasis was used… or rather the term 'Negative Theology' was used, by Thomas Aquinas to define for us the proof of God's existence.

SMERDYAKOV. Defining what God is by what he isn't?

IVAN. Theologians love that sort of shit! Let's now examine God with apophatic inquiry, shall we?

SMERDYAKOV *actually shivers with excitement.*

To describe God as both omnipotent and omniscient, were that combination even possible, imposes man's notion of what a spirit may be on God. To imagine God existing in many forms would be to deny Him His very divinity, and so, 'God is not a multiple being.' Therefore, we can assume He is a single man. One cannot say that God painted the Earth in all its splendour to condemn man to lifetimes of moral cross-examination, because that would suggest a meddlesome malevolence… and so God is into interior decoration. A single man into interior decoration?

SMERDYAKOV. God is not a heterosexual man.

IVAN. You understand my point?

SMERDYAKOV. Yes, I think so. But you're being humorous.

IVAN. Am I?

SMERDYAKOV. By implying God is gay. He's not gay, is He?

IVAN. And why wouldn't He be gay?

SMERDYAKOV. Because He has a big white beard.

IVAN *is unsure whether* SMERDYAKOV *is making a joke.*

IVAN. Right.

Slight pause.

The actual point I'm making is that Thomas Aquinas wasted a lifetime trying to define God through Negative Theology.

SMERDYAKOV. Right!

IVAN. Aquinas promoted the idea that the Divine is ineffable... it's a feeling, an aspect of existence that is too profound to be described in words... it can only be known by the individual internally. Vague enough for you!?

SMERDYAKOV. Yes, very vague. Preposterous.

IVAN. And that, Smerdyakov, is faith... is belief. Faith is... truly... a terrible mystery to me.

SMERDYAKOV. It's terrible to you because you have no beliefs?

IVAN. I have many beliefs, of course I have.

SMERDYAKOV. Yes.

Slight pause.

IVAN. I believe that man is capable of creating new forms of art, new sciences, new religions, new politics. That man will continually reinvent. Even you, Smerdyakov, under my guidance perhaps, even you may take this bottle of brandy... may design and engineer a rocket that would fire the brandy into outer space, for whatever stupid reason. It would circle the globe for years. And we would write articles about this bottle... and other people would write articles about our articles. And we would lie in these articles and soon people would become fixated by this brandy bottle. They would allow the bottle to make decisions for them, they would pray to it, they'd build churches to it. On the altar there'd be a sculpture of the bottle's son... a small miniature bottle – the type you find in mini-bars... his liquid drunk, his label peeled, his glass body crucified. People would weep for that miniature bottle. 'Brandyism' would be born. It would sweep the world... and all because of me and you. All because two men stayed up late. Two men planned it. We gave our life to it. Our ideas... made things. Two men changed the world.

Long pause.

SMERDYAKOV *has been holding his breath. He may fall over.*

22

I've a very important meeting with Katerina Ivanovna in the morning. Run me a bath. A scented bath.

IVAN *leaves*. SMERDYAKOV *scrambles and rewinds the tape. He hits play.*

IVAN (*recorded*). That man will continually reinvent. Even you, Smerdyakov, under my guidance perhaps, even you...

SMERDYAKOV *stops the tape.*

He stares at his hand. His hand is sweating.

He rubs it on his trousers.

Suddenly a moaning, screaming sound. SMERDYAKOV *looks towards the sound, then exits to avoid* FYODOR.

Scene Eight

FYODOR *rolls into the space gripping his head. His body writhes around and we can hear him mumbling and seemingly chastising himself and calling himself a 'Bad man!' It's unclear whether he is awake or not.*

We hear GRUSHENKA *singing the first verse of 'You Don't Own Me' by Lesley Gore. She is lit as if in a cabaret club.*

FYODOR (*whispers*). Grushenka, sweetheart?

GRUSHENKA. Yes, Fyodor.

FYODOR. We will sing tonight.

Slight pause.

GRUSHENKA. And it will be fun.

FYODOR *smiles.*

(*As fact.*) Hearts will be broken.

GRUSHENKA *sings.*

During the song, FYODOR *realises he is bleeding heavily from his stomach. He looks at the blood on his hands and stumbles offstage.*

Scene Nine

Back at the Travelodge.

MITYA. It's Grushenka I love! Katerina is a goddess. I could never be the man she deserves to have. She will always be a beautiful painting to me. To be admired, adored, to investigate... a painting I have no right to look at... let alone own... But Grushenka! She is me! She is heart and body. One touch from her and I'm reduced to jelly! Each second away from her is a torture. Fuck it! Where is she?! Does she love him? Does she love our father?! Tell me! I need to find out where this new club is! I need to find her before it's too late! Before he takes Grushenka from me!

He holds a letter out to ALYOSHA.

I want you to go to Katerina, return this love letter she gave me and tell her I will never see her again. Say to that brave beautiful woman... 'He kisses your hand. It's over.' Tell her precisely that! It has to be you, Alyosha, and only you! You are my only hope! Promise me! Go! Say you'll go! What I'm doing is releasing her! It's Ivan she needs to be with! You mention her name to Ivan and he's suddenly got a pulse! He's in love with Katerina and she deserves a good man! Go to her! Break my engagement! Free her of me, for me... free her for Ivan's heart, Alyosha! Say you'll go! Say it!

ALYOSHA *takes the love letter.*

I swear the money will be returned to Katerina! I'll work for that money if I have to! Today I will work! We are on a mission! You to free me of Katerina and me to raise this money and find Grushenka! I may be an insect, but right now I'm reborn! I'm brightly coloured, I'm in flight! We're taking to the dawn! Me and you! We are masters of our destiny, of this brand new day! To Katerina's! Take flight! FLY!

MITYA *flings* ALYOSHA *into the air, and slumps back into his chair, spent.*

Scene Ten

Rather gracelessly, ALYOSHA *lands on the floor with a thump. He stands, opens his backpack and takes out a sock.*

He's already sewn buttons onto the sock to make eyes. He mimics FATHER ZOSIMA*'s voice and tries to find his words as he works the puppet.*

ALYOSHA. Be strong, Alyosha. Live your life in faith. Love others unconditionally. Begin with family.

ALYOSHA *carefully places his* FATHER ZOSIMA PUPPET *back in his backpack.*

Scene Eleven

Music is heard gently playing in the background.

KATERINA *is watching something happening inside a small wooden box. It's an amazing clockwork mechanism of some sort, probably musical.*

IVAN *stands behind* KATERINA, *looking at her with complete devotion.*

KATERINA. It's lovely.

IVAN. It's as close a representation of yourself as I could imagine in wood. Insightful, precise, entertaining and luminous.

KATERINA. And you really made it?

IVAN. Yes! Hewn from a log I pass on my walk every day. The clockwork mechanism was the real achievement. Damn fiddly!

KATERINA *turns and looks at him.*

KATERINA. And what's that smell?

Pause.

IVAN. Me. I had a scented bath earlier.

KATERINA. Oh.

IVAN*'s unsure what 'Oh' means. He's rattled.*

(*A little hesitant.*) So can I speak to you about something very important?

IVAN. You will speak, I will listen, you will stop speaking, I will respond!

KATERINA. Let's sit.

They sit.

Pause as KATERINA *composes herself and* IVAN *waits.*

Ivan. I've been trying to pull together the bits of me that have been lied to, been used, been betrayed. Tried to bundle up emotions that feel shredded, stamped on… It's impossible for me to fully understand the extent of my suffering, but it exists and it needs gathering… it needs… 'direction', I call it. So I thought it was important to find some words that would steer me into and through this new direction. And the words that burned into me… that… in even saying these… and they are terribly old words, Ivan… but with these two words I can see a purpose to me… the words I see are 'honour' and 'duty'. (*Slight pause.*) Honour this man. Never abandon this man. Even if this man hates me, betrays me, I will follow him always. And he may tell me to leave and I will leave but I will watch over this man all my life. And when he needs a friend, a sister, I will come to him and be his sister. This is my religion, my quest. He is my devotion. (*Slight pause.*) And even if… and I feel he may well do, Ivan… even if Mitya breaks our engagement and follows this bitch, Grushenka… honour and duty will guide me through any heartache, I'm sure of it. There is no heartache for me. Mitya is my charge, my vocation, my purpose. My whole life I will be a machine for his happiness. I will…

IVAN (*crushed*). Stop it!

IVAN *tries to scramble a response. As he does, he wants to touch her.*

Let me… gather. What you don't… My brother… is… While I don't fully understand… while I can see this… Your what?… the word… 'honour'. His barbarism. His… There is no… never will there be a more… He will torture you. He will see your suffering, Katya. You deserve… Don't. Don't. Listen. We… what we are…

KATERINA. I'm not explaining myself properly! You may think that I'm clinging on, that I still have hope, that I will only live if I feel that I am saving mine and Mitya's romance. I mustn't think about that now. I can't think about that any more! I'm not thinking about that impossibly slim chance! So listen again.

IVAN *has to stand. He's breathless.*

I will be the ground he walks on. I will be the steps he climbs, the door he opens, the hallway he enters, the banister he places his hand on. I will be the shirt he takes off, the rug the shirt has fallen on. I will be the bed he lies on, the sheets that cover his back, the pillow his hand clenches in ecstasy, his toilet, the tissue paper he wipes himself with. The air Mitya breathes, the air that dries his brow. I am the ruffled bed he returns to from the bathroom. His darkness as he lies back beside Grushenka. A darkness that soothes his soul, that calms his breath, that finds him peace, that gives him sleep...

ALYOSHA *bursts through the door pursued by a vicious dog.*

He closes the door fast. KATERINA *goes to him.*

Alyosha! Did the dogs frighten you? I breed them to be critical.

IVAN. I never knew you bred dogs.

KATERINA. My life is very full.

Pause. ALYOSHA *stands there in shock.*

(*To* ALYOSHA, *brightly.*) Well, hello!

KATERINA *kisses his cheek.*

Look at you! You look lovely! We've had some coffee and croissants. There are biscuits. Would you like a sponge-finger? Maybe a glass of milk? I can't believe there's three years between Ivan and you! Isn't he young-looking, Ivan? Ivan? And what news? Is it true about Father Zosima?! His miraculous and glorious soul! Don't speak! There's something very important I need to tell you first... Let me speak. I will speak. First listen. Then you respond. Let's sit.

ALYOSHA *has taken out* KATERINA*'s love letter to return it to her. She chooses not to see it.*

It concerns Mitya. It concerns a new role I see for myself in his life. A role strengthened with unwavering duty. Regardless of whether he loves me or not, whether he hates me, is repulsed by me… I will be his everything. From the rug he walks on to the elements that surround him, Alyosha. Perhaps even invisible for him. I'm particles of the tiniest matter. I'm atoms charged with positively charged protons, a nucleus of pure honour. I will be his Universe. I will align the Cosmos and steer his fate to happiness. Forgive me for saying this, Alyosha, but I will be a god which he can pray to. In my omnipresence I will strengthen his resolve to make good, to find himself peace, to be the man I know he can be…

ALYOSHA *looks down on the love letter. It seems pointless to give it to her.* KATERINA *continues.*

I could have found much easier words. I'm sorry. But that's my decision and Ivan fully approves.

IVAN *comes back to life.*

IVAN. What? Oh, yes! Of course! As ideas go… it's a good one! A really…? It's great! I don't know what to say! I'm completely lost for words.

KATERINA. Well, in which case…

IVAN. Actually I've just found some! (*Slight pause.*) Katerina Ivanovna. Anyone else would be slightly embarrassed by that faux poetic imagery falling from that delicious mouth of yours… but you're not embarrassed. Because you really… feel it. It's emotionally true to you. To anyone else, promising to be a rug would be a metaphor too far… but you can actually see yourself pinned to the floor with Mitya's heels in your back. Perhaps you've got a non-slip underlay rug velcroed to your front to protect your beloved Mitya from slipping and cracking his fucking skull open. Very wise. (*Slight pause.*) I can see you as a chair… as of now, I can certainly see you as darkness. (*Slight pause.*) This terrible lie you tell yourself as you cling to a dead love… now disguised by 'honour' and 'duty'. And tell me… this 'new role'… it's really going to fulfil you?

He begins to applaud her.

Then it's a triumph! A genius!

He stops.

Sadly I won't be here to see you fall further. I have to return to Moscow! Bye bye!

KATERINA *intercepts* IVAN *as he tries to exit.*

KATERINA. What?! (*Slight pause.*) But this is great news! Though obviously I'm sad you're leaving. But maybe you can deliver this package to my very elderly aunt?

KATERINA *hands* IVAN *a parcel in the shape of a dog.*

IVAN. I would love to! I can't think of anything else I would rather do than to pull myself away from the intelligentsia and deliver this strangely shaped package to your very elderly aunt! Any more chores you need doing while I'm not living? Cleaning the fucking kennels, maybe!? Would you like to etch her address into my forehead?

KATERINA. That won't be necessary, it's written on the parcel here.

ALYOSHA *suddenly takes* IVAN's *hand, then* KATERINA's *hand and tries to join them together.*

KATERINA *suddenly smashes* ALYOSHA *in the face.*

WHAT ARE YOU DOING? WHAT ARE YOU DOING? Who do you think you are, you religious idiot! What do you know of life?! Three weeks out of the monastery! You're a boy! How dare you come into my house and tell me who I love and who I don't!? Look at you in your silly little clothes! You're a fucking child! GET OUT! GET OUT!

ALYOSHA *is reeling. His mouth starts to bleed.*

Long pause.

IVAN. Had you cast yourself as an angel of our destiny, Alyosha? Seen a way to settle the rivalry between Mitya and father. Trick Katerina into loving me and free Mitya to love Grushenka. In your childish understanding of life and love it must have appeared simple to you. (*Slight pause.*) Well, she's never loved me. How could she? She knows I love her... I've never said the word 'love'... but she knew. She doesn't even want me as a friend. She brings me here to revenge all the suffering she takes from Mitya. All I ever hear is the love you have for him. The

more he insults you, the more you love him. So lie to yourself
every moment and see what I care! How must it be to live with
your fucking pride? (*Pause. Softly.*) How can I still want the
love of a woman I pity and now hate so much? (*Slight pause.*)
I'm going now! I've said everything. But I'd like to leave you
with a little poem! It's by Catullus. (*Pause.*) *Odi et amo. Quare
id faciam, fortasse requiris? Nescio, sed fieri sentio et excrucior.*
(*Pause.*) Now... let's not kiss! Fuck it!

He leaves to the sound of howling dogs.

Pause. ALYOSHA *looks at* KATERINA *who is still and
stunned.*

KATERINA (*hard*). Shush! (*Slight pause.*) What just happened
didn't happen. Find Grushenka. Tell her I want to speak with
her about Mitya. We need to meet tonight. Do that for me! It's
the least you can do. Go! Go!

ALYOSHA *leaves the light.*

Scene Twelve

SMERDYAKOV *appears in the space breathless, wearing a
bonnet and a paint-splattered apron. In his hands he holds large
pieces of paper with frantic black-ink drawings on them.*

From nowhere, MITYA *appears. He grabs* SMERDYAKOV *by
the throat.*

MITYA. This party... where and when, idiot?

MITYA *steps away from him. He's holding one of*
SMERDYAKOV's *drawings. He rips it to pieces.*

SMERDYAKOV *calmly walks behind the puppet booth.*

Scene Thirteen

KATERINA *places her hand into the musical box and smashes the lid down on it.*

She opens her mouth to scream, but the scream is SMERDYAKOV*'s.*

He appears above his screen, framed by a toy theatre. He is holding a ukulele.

SMERDYAKOV. This is the ballad of the Shrieker, Fyodor's second wife, and mother of Ivan and Alyosha!

He begins to play.

Oooooh!! Look at them! (*Etc.*)

Ivan is seven and Alyosha just four.

He lets out a piercing shriek.

And that sound you hear is the Shrieker on the other side of
the door.
Fyodor had a whore in the house last night
And made his wife watch... again.
Things like that would bring on her hysteria,
Which tired the life out of him.
Then one night she stepped up from her prayers,
And shrieked and shrieked for a week or two.
Ivan was seven and Alyosha just four
When the Shrieker was dragged through her fine front door.
She shrieked all the way to her grave, they said.
This was the look on Fyodor's face at the moment
He was informed of her death.

SMERDYAKOV *shows a disinterested 'look'.*

He did say, 'Those innocent eyes cut my soul like a razor!'
But that was a long time ago,
Now she's six feet under.
Ivan read books and books and books and books
Packaged up and passed from school to school
By guardians who found him... sullen
Which was all too true.
And Alyosha with his polished little 'angel face'

Skipped through a sequence of schools
Till he entered those monastery gates,
Slipped into his cassock... Oooooooooh, nice!
And his make-believe dog collar,
What a fucking mutt!
Here they are sitting around,
Not saying a lot;
The angel Alyosha and the sullen Ivan,
The sons of the Shrieker.

I thank you.

Scene Fourteen

SMERDYAKOV *finishes his performance and wheels off his puppet booth.*

FYODOR *appears from behind a screen, costumed as a Turkish pasha.*

A long pause as ALYOSHA *and* IVAN *look at him.* ALYOSHA *looks bashed, bruised and bloodied.*

IVAN (*to* FYODOR). Is there a reason why you're dressed like Ali Baba?

FYODOR. A very good reason. What do you make of the tan?

IVAN. Thought you were Omar Sharif.

FYODOR. Out of a bottle!

IVAN. You appeared out of a bottle?

FYODOR. The tan! It's fake!

IVAN. Well I never!

FYODOR. Thought we'd spice up tonight's opening by making it fancy dress! Grushenka will love it!

IVAN. Great.

FYODOR. Worth postponing your trip to Moscow? Say you'll come! It won't be the same!

IVAN. I'll leave in the morning as happy as a clam who's been injected with happy serum.

FYODOR. Good man! And as long as Mitya knows what's good for him the evening will pass without incident. Though who might know what Mitya is thinking, hey, Alyosha?! (*To* IVAN.) Ohhh, doesn't he look bashed and bruised?! Hard being out in the real world, was it? Tough day? Oh, my poor little angel. Give your pasha a little hug.

FYODOR hugs ALYOSHA in a tight grip. He's really hurting him.

(*Suddenly.*) Why are you helping Mitya over me? A man who stole three grand from his fiancée! And you trying to get Ivan to fall in love with Katerina and her with him so Mitya can be with Grushenka!

FYODOR suddenly has ALYOSHA by the throat.

Did you not return to Mitya's Travelodge, speak with him, define your plan and set about ruining me!? Don't you even think about lying to me, boy! I love you and you betrayed my love! Grushenka is mine! Mitya remains engaged to Katerina... Ivan is... Ivan is Ivan!

IVAN. And what is Ivan?

FYODOR. An island. A tomb!

Almost spitting in ALYOSHA's face.

Now, Father Liar... WHERE! IS! MITYA!?

MITYA enters fast and dives on FYODOR. FYODOR flies across the floor.

MITYA (*calls*). Grushenka! Grushenka!

ALYOSHA grabs MITYA.

FYODOR. Lackey, get me a knife so I can protect myself!

SMERDYAKOV doesn't move.

SMERDYAKOV. The knives are in the dishwasher, boss.

MITYA. With my hands I'll rip you apart, insect!

FYODOR. Hold him!

FYODOR's nose is bleeding.

MITYA. Grushenka!

FYODOR. Out of my house, you thief!

MITYA is suddenly free and knocks FYODOR *to the ground.*

He starts to stamp on FYODOR's *face.*

MITYA. WHERE! ARE! YOU! KEEP! ING! HER!

FYODOR. Nowhere!

MITYA starts to strangle him.

MITYA. I know it's tonight! I know it's in Mokroe! That cheap
little room behind the ballroom!

FYODOR. You won't get past the dogs!

MITYA's maybe killing him.

ALYOSHA (*screams*). NO!

ALYOSHA runs at MITYA *and floors him.*

FYODOR, MITYA *and* ALYOSHA *scramble on the ground.*

IVAN calmly turns to SMERDYAKOV *and holds out his
Advocaat.*

IVAN. Brandy.

SMERDYAKOV takes the Advocaat and hands IVAN *the bottle
of brandy.*

IVAN downs the remains of the bottle.

ALYOSHA stands, holding FYODOR *and* MITYA.

ALYOSHA. ENOUGH! NOW STOP! STOP! STOP IT!

FYODOR and MITYA *back away from each other.*

We are a family starved of love! With Christ's guidance you can
settle these differences, now please stop it!

Pause.

MITYA *slowly backs away.*

MITYA (*quiet*). There's no room for Christ between him and me. It will be settled our way tonight in Mokroe.

FYODOR. But still, nothing's changed. Still need that three thousand to free you of Katerina. You're fucked.

MITYA. Then hearts will be broken. Lives taken.

MITYA turns and leaves.

ALYOSHA. Mitya, please! We need to sit and talk!

Pause.

FYODOR (*re: his bloodied blouse*). I'm going to lose my deposit on this. Bastard!

IVAN (*to* ALYOSHA). Why do you always bring Christ into the room?

Pause.

ALYOSHA *turns to* IVAN. IVAN*'s beginning to boil.*

ALYOSHA. I don't ever bring Christ here, Ivan. (*Pause.*) Anyway Christ is here. He's in each of us. Even a Karamazov.

ALYOSHA *gathers himself and reaches for his backpack.*

IVAN. Of course, all this sinning is His doing. The blame is His. It's hard to acknowledge or want such a Christ inside you.

Pause.

ALYOSHA (*tentative*). I don't understand what you're talking about.

IVAN. The blame is His. This 'free will' He's given us.

Slight pause.

ALYOSHA (*about to open his backpack*). Ivan, please...

IVAN. Maybe it was those forty days wandering in the desert, maybe His malnourished brain had clouded His judgment or perhaps just sharpened it. Whether He was demented or He knowingly ruined us... He has placed us all into the hands of Satan. It's all His doing and any sinning in this house has Christ's hands all over it. More brandy, lackey!

SMERDYAKOV *hands him another bottle of brandy.*

ALYOSHA. Ivan, I'm sorry about Katerina.

IVAN *is furious he's mentioned her here. He gulps back some of the bottle.*

IVAN. You bring Christ into this house and I'll place Him in the dock.

FYODOR. Go on, Ivan!

SMERDYAKOV *begins to record* IVAN's *tirade.*

IVAN. When asked to turn stones to bread… an act that would see mankind follow him… Jesus Christ rejected the offer. 'What is freedom worth if obedience could be bought with bread?', His pious reasoning. And we're promised the Bread of Heaven, but how could that compare to earthly bread to the minds of the weak? What is the one thing that humanity craves?

SMERDYAKOV (*bleating*). Belief! Belief!

IVAN. Something to worship. There is nothing more certain in life than bread! But to give us this choice… this impossible free will… He's given us disaffection, confusion, un-fucking-happiness… Christ-like misery!

IVAN *drinks more brandy.*

Secondly… when Satan asked Christ to show him a miracle, to throw Himself off a cliff and be caught by the angels… Christ stood there all quiet. And maybe He doubted God at that point. Maybe He pictured His body snapping on the rocks… the angels standing by, shrugging their shoulders… perhaps He had those doubts.

But Christ refused Satan in a more calculated way. Like in an instant he could see this parable and how it would be handed down through generations. 'Mankind should never beg for miracles!' But we… the weak ones… are not so much looking for God but the miraculous. In not seeing it from the invisible God… we'll search out new miracles, new beliefs… we'll find it in witchcraft, in sorcery, in brandy, in heroin, in whores. Man is much too weak to use choice to find his salvation. I mean, look at the fucking state of us all!

IVAN *takes more brandy, as if he's poisoning himself.*

And then that last temptation, to declare Himself sole ruler of
His Kingdom. He could have given us someone to worship,
someone to keep a morality for... He could have united us all.
Who can rule mankind if not the man who holds their conscience and their bread in His hands? Is there anything more
seductive for man than the freedom to choose between right and
wrong? And is there anything that gives him more suffering
than that choice? Is it any surprise we've been left chatting to
Satan when he gives us bread, Alyosha! At least he fattens us
up. Denied spirituality and love, the world says, 'You have
needs? Satisfy them!' That is our freedom! Satan is in this house
saying, 'Satisfy yourself!'... while Christ sits with God, glo-
rying in their fucking chaos, speaking love and forgiveness
through the mouths of priests?! Life-ignorant priests! How dare
you be in this house, be part of our day and speak of sinning
when it is all Jesus Christ's doing! It is His!

IVAN *is finished.*

FYODOR *laughs a little.*

SMERDYAKOV *is in awe. He speaks a footnote into his
microphone.*

SMERDYAKOV. Ivan speaks of the impossible burden of choice
and free will. Jesus Christ is blamed.

IVAN *is shaking.*

Long pause.

ALYOSHA *begins hesitantly.*

ALYOSHA. That's how the world sees its freedom, it's true. I
know what this world has become, Ivan. I'm not that ignorant of
how we are... (*Pause.*) The spiritual world, the higher half of
man's being, has been rejected and in its place man is satisfying
his base needs, his foolish desires, his base nature distorted and
displayed for everyone to see. The proof for me has been in this
day. It's certainly in this house. (*Pause.*) To have cars, property,
mistresses, servants to clean, servants to honour their every
want... is now considered a necessity. So you sacrifice life...
you sacrifice the love of mankind. Instead of serving brotherly
love, families have fallen into dispute. Oneness of people is an

idea at best mocked... it's ignored! (*Pause*.) How do you turn
from a life of selfishness to even care about the whole? In
amassing more and more things, man has less joy. This is not
Christ's doing, Ivan. Freedom to follow does not mean freedom
to debase oneself...

IVAN *scoffs*. ALYOSHA *stops. A crisis of confidence suddenly.*

So emm... So if you could please... please give me... just a few
moments... and perhaps... Father Zosima's words may unite us
as brothers... as family.

ALYOSHA *begins to perform some sort of ritual for the emer-
gence of the* FATHER ZOSIMA PUPPET. *The* PUPPET *ludi-
crously bursts out from a hole above* ALYOSHA's *heart.*

FYODOR, IVAN *and* SMERDYAKOV *are, naturally, dumb-
founded.*

Long pause.

(*Speaking as* FATHER ZOSIMA.) Be not forgetful of prayer.
For when you pray and when that prayer is sincere, it will give
you fresh courage.

FYODOR *bursts out laughing. Stops.*

FYODOR. Carry on. (*Slight pause*.) Sorry, Father Zosima!

Pause. ALYOSHA *continues.*

ALYOSHA (*speaking as* FATHER ZOSIMA). Love all God's cre-
ation, love the animals, love the plants, love everything. Love
children especially... for they are sinless like the angels...

FYODOR (*suddenly*). What the fuck is this we're watching!? Oh,
you've got some madness inside of you!

During the following exchange, FYODOR *grapples with*
ALYOSHA *and the sock puppet tearing it from* ALYOSHA's
chest.

Zosima, is it really you!? You look terrible, Holy Father!

ALYOSHA. I'm not ready to let him go!

FYODOR. It's a sock!? Fucking hell, Ivan! He's lost it!

ALYOSHA. Stop it!

FYODOR. He's dead!

ALYOSHA. He is still with me!

FYODOR. Holy Jesus…!

IVAN. Let it go, Fyodor!

FYODOR. He's dead, Alyosha! Zosima is dead!

ALYOSHA. No!

FYODOR. Is this what you've been doing in your bedroom these past three weeks since you buried Zosima!? He's in the ground! The man was a fucking idiot! A pompous senile fuck! His words are dead, Alyosha! It's all dead! Family? Dead! Goodness? Dead!

FYODOR *animates the* PUPPET, *doing its voice.*

LOVE THE FUCKING PLANTS! LOVE CHILDREN! LOVE ME! LOVE GOD! I'LL FUCKING LOVE YOU!

FYODOR*'s lost it. He starts fucking the sock puppet.*

FYODOR *looks at* ALYOSHA *who has started to cry. He flings the puppet on the ground.*

How long to go till my Opening Night Party, Smerdyakov!?

SMERDYAKOV. An hour, boss.

FYODOR. Time to show some Karamazov colour then! That Kara-mazov insect! I've not got dressed for nothing, have I? (*Slight pause.*) To Mokroe… and God help us!

Scene Fifteen

We watch each character prepare for their outing to FYODOR*'s club.*

MITYA *finds and loads his gun.*

SMERDYAKOV *drops* FYODOR*'s old clothes in front of* ALYOSHA.

ALYOSHA *begins to dress in them.*

KATERINA *is bandaging her hand.*

IVAN *is talking to the devil.*

GRUSHENKA *is packing all her things into a suitcase.*

SMERDYAKOV *is dressing himself up as a butler.*

During this sequence the furniture in the space is pushed aside by FYODOR *until the stage is a more open, bare space.*

End of Act One.

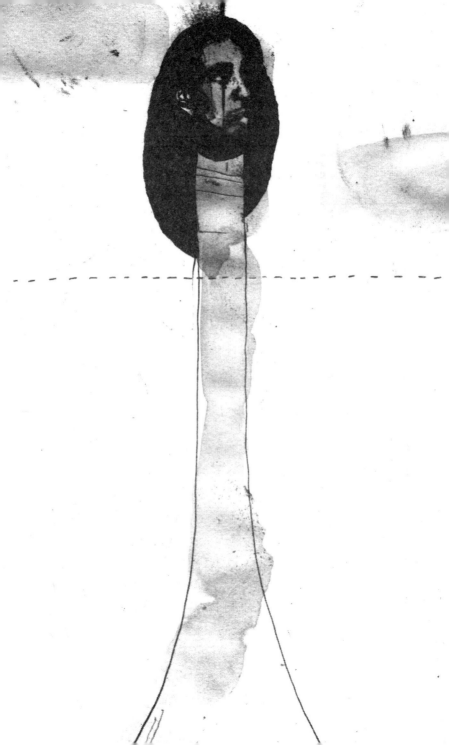

ACT TWO

Scene One

We are in FYODOR*'s club. Public Enemy's 'Son of a Bush' plays and each of the characters – apart from* ALYOSHA *– are wildly 'dancing' and setting up the mood for the rest of the evening.*

They are all in fancy dress.

FYODOR *is dressed as a pasha,* MITYA *as a gorilla,* IVAN *as Superman,* ALYOSHA *as his father,* SMERDYAKOV *as a butler,* KATERINA *as Juliette Binoche's nurse in* The English Patient.

Scene Two

FYODOR *and* GRUSHENKA *perform 'The Damsel and the Island King' to the tune of Screamin' Jay Hawkins' 'I Put A Spell On You'.*

During this they pull MITYA, *'the gorilla', into the act and unmask him.*

The performance ends and GRUSHENKA *speaks to* MITYA, *the moment existing 'out of time'.*

Scene Three

GRUSHENKA. We were once in a bedroom no more than one hundred metres away from here. Above the ballroom.

MITYA. Right.

GRUSHENKA. Thirty minutes previous to that we met for the first time. It was a very hot night and they opened the ballroom doors into the car park and it was impossible to tell whether you were inside or outside the ballroom. The temperature was the same and the crowd moved in and out of the doors, all languid, all happily drunk.

MITYA. I'm moving through that crowd as they move into one another, ebbing up and down, hands down pants, up skirts, spit passed back and forth.

GRUSHENKA. I could feel hands around my waist, bodies pressing against me, the music inside us all and I was thinking… this is my most favourite place on Earth.

MITYA. People focused on vice, planning their conquests, rehearsing their moves. I only want for the outside. For a breeze. Something to freshen me up, to replace me with a new me. (*Slight pause.*) I feel alone with Katerina's three thousand burning in my pockets. I'm a thief. A terrible thief.

GRUSHENKA. My feet lift off the ground and I can see you in front and you're standing still.

MITYA. I could hear my insect in my stomach. He was joined by other insects and they were scratching me badly. Reminding me what terrible thievery I had done. But I see you. You're moving towards me on this tide.

GRUSHENKA. And your arm is around me suddenly and you're pulling me in tight to you. And our lips are only millimetres away from one another and your breath is on my lips and I can smell a mint. A Trebor Softmint?

MITYA. Yeah.

GRUSHENKA. And it's certain you're going to kiss me.

MITYA. And it's certain you're going to kiss me.

And now 'back in the club'.

I've been looking for you all day.

GRUSHENKA. And where were you before today?

MITYA. Benidorm.

GRUSHENKA *laughs a little. She then notices that* MITYA *is holding a gun.*

GRUSHENKA. Is that real?

MITYA. Promise me the night will end the way I've prayed for it to end.

GRUSHENKA. Or what?

MITYA. Or I'll shoot myself, I swear I will.

GRUSHENKA. Drink and enjoy yourself, Mitya!

GRUSHENKA *goes to leave*.

MITYA. Aren't we going to talk?!

GRUSHENKA *turns to him*.

GRUSHENKA. I'll call you soon! Now, drink! (*Slight pause*.) You're here!

GRUSHENKA *leaves*. MITYA *quickly places the gun back in his gorilla suit*.

Scene Four

FYODOR *talks at* SMERDYAKOV.

FYODOR. Look at this place, Smerdyakov! I was always a great one for an opportunity, for finding a niche. As a child I shunned the cowboys... for me it was all about the Indians! You could have a pack of cowboys, but I'd always stay with my own tribe. Even if I were a tribe of one which I often was, I didn't care. I'd ride into town with all manner of abuse flying in my face, but fuck 'em! I was an individual! They broke the mould when they made me! I was an eight-year-old, full-blooded Cherokee Indian! You'll always remember your first scalp. Mine was a six-year-old cocky Thalidomide who got the better of me in a gun fight! I pinned him to the ground, held down his flippers and spat in his eyes!

He jumps on SMERDYAKOV*'s back*.

'Don't you mock me!!' Come on, Smerdyakov, run, boy, run! Run! Run! Run! Run! Run! Run! Run!

He rides SMERDYAKOV.

Scene Five

ALYOSHA *and* KATERINA *are in mid-conversation.*

ALYOSHA. 'He kisses your hand. It's over.'

KATERINA. He was definite with the words?

ALYOSHA. Very.

KATERINA. Right. 'He kisses your hand. It's over.' I see. (*Slight pause.*) Had Mitya said those words in passing like he was busy doing something else and the words dribbled from his mouth and were expressed with a meaningless wave of the hand... well, that would be the end of him... the end of everything! I'd cut his cock off and nail him to a cross.

ALYOSHA*'s shocked. He has no way of responding to that.*

But because he insisted on those very words and he was definite that you repeat exactly the same words to me... well, that suggests that he was excited, that he made a decision and he was frightened of that decision. He wasn't walking away from me with a resolute step... but leaping headlong. The whole phrasing suggests bravado! And if so... he's not altogether lost, is he?! He's only in despair and I can still save him! (*Slight pause.*) Now, to Grushenka! Organise our meeting! Go!

She pushes ALYOSHA *towards* GRUSHENKA*'s dressing room.*

Scene Six

ALYOSHA *passes through the dance floor with* KATERINA *following.*

IVAN *very nearly collides with* KATERINA.

Inches apart and they try to step out of each other's way. This awkward side-stepping quickly ratchets up into a small bit of choreography.

Eventually, KATERINA *passes.* IVAN*'s heart constricts. He clutches it.*

Scene Seven

ALYOSHA *leaves as* KATERINA *comes face to face with* GRUSHENKA.

KATERINA. Congratulations on your performance.

GRUSHENKA. Thank you.

KATERINA. I don't know how you do it. I once had to imper-sonate Madonna at a charity event. I chafed that badly they had to wheel me home in a wheelchair.

GRUSHENKA. Did you want me to have that information?

KATERINA. No. Do you know who I am?

GRUSHENKA. Yes.

Scene Eight

ALYOSHA *marches from* GRUSHENKA*'s dressing room and is stopped by* MITYA.

MITYA. 'He kisses your hand. It's over.' You said those words?

ALYOSHA. Just talk to her and break the engagement. You do that… you're free.

MITYA. But I must pay her the money! Aren't you going to help me?!

ALYOSHA (*explodes*). You're not my responsibility, Mitya!

ALYOSHA *goes to leave, but is stopped as he sees* FYODOR *lying on the ground in front of him. He seems to be having sex with the floor.* SMERDYAKOV *films him.*

The three brothers are suddenly around, looking down at their degenerate father.

IVAN (*to his brothers, with dread*). Isn't that a Karamazov? We don't so much live but burn up. It's not air we breathe but pure oxygen. We are all wired differently in style and tone, us brothers, and yet we're plugged into the same life force. His life force.

FYODOR*'s up fast. He grabs* SMERDYAKOV.

FYODOR. Didn't you send invites out? It's fucking empty!

SMERDYAKOV. How do you mean, boss?

FYODOR. Well, friends and family for a start!

SMERDYAKOV. But you don't have any friends. This is it.

FYODOR (*snaps*). So what have you come as, duffer?!

SMERDYAKOV. A butler.

FYODOR. Make yourself useful then! Give me some atmosphere!

SMERDYAKOV *goes to the sound system and puts on some dance music.*

FYODOR *goes centre stage and begins to dance. The others are drawn into a choreographed dance.*

Towards the end, GRUSHENKA *goes back to her dressing room.*

Scene Nine

KATERINA *grabs* ALYOSHA *by the hand. She brings him back to* GRUSHENKA.

KATERINA. It's important you're here to see this. I regret punching you in the face. This is your reward!

KATERINA *holds* GRUSHENKA *and starts covering her face with kisses.* ALYOSHA *watches.*

You see, you see, you see, you see, you see, you see, you see…

KATERINA *gives her one last big kiss on the lips.*

Pause.

GRUSHENKA *calmly redoes her lipstick while* KATERINA *buzzes with excitement.*

We have just talked and what is clear is that Mitya will never marry Grushenka! For one thing, it's not love but passion he has for her, and a Karamazov passion can barely outlive an afternoon…!

Both KATERINA *and* GRUSHENKA *laugh –* KATERINA *a little too ecstatic.*

And for another thing… she won't marry him anyway… and this is what we have just discussed all of five minutes ago, right? Right?!

GRUSHENKA. As you say.

KATERINA. You see!

ALYOSHA. That's good.

KATERINA. It's great news!

ALYOSHA. It is.

GRUSHENKA. It is.

KATERINA. Thank you for putting us together, Alyosha.

ALYOSHA. Pleasure.

GRUSHENKA. The brother loved by everyone. You look a little sad. Will I comfort you?

ALYOSHA *doesn't know how to respond to this obvious come-on.*

ALYOSHA. Goodbye.

KATERINA *takes* GRUSHENKA*'s hand and stands beside her, blocking* ALYOSHA*'s exit.*

KATERINA. Isn't she an angel? You can see why men are bewitched by her. She's beautiful but also strong, noble, kind…

GRUSHENKA. All words to describe you. All that and more.

KATERINA. We have felt terrible heartache, haven't we?

Slight pause.

GRUSHENKA (*careful*). Yes.

KATERINA. Yes, we have. We were only eighteen years old and we were ready to make every sacrifice for a fickle unworthy man. We were a soft-hearted, silly creature, weren't we? This man left us and he married and soon he had long forgotten about that young, proud woman that we would always be. Recently his lovely wife died and he wrote us a letter and he is coming here tonight, Alyosha! We will have our reunion with this man tonight... by the fire-exit door strewn with shit and condoms... we will have this stunningly romantic rendezvous there tonight! He will take us away from here. Far far far away! We have always loved this man and will love him for all of our life. Grushenka will be happy again. For the last five years she's been a wretched creature, through some fault of her own, known more for her degenerate whoring than her performing...

GRUSHENKA. Please. (*Slight pause.*) You're defending me too kindly now.

KATERINA *kisses her full on the lips*.

You kissing me like that is not going to make me blush.

KATERINA. Then you misunderstand me because it is not my intention to make you blush.

Pause.

More steel to GRUSHENKA *now.*

GRUSHENKA. And you have also misunderstood me. Because I'm not as good as you may think I am. I have a very sneaky heart, you see. From the first night I met Mitya, I infatuated him...

KATERINA. But now you will save him!

GRUSHENKA. Will I?

Slight pause.

KATERINA. Well, what we just discussed. You will tell him that you love another man and that you'll be leaving with that man tonight. Mitya will be mine. You gave me your word.

GRUSHENKA. No I didn't. You just kept on talking about it until you believed I said it...

KATERINA. But you promised me...

GRUSHENKA. I didn't promise you anything. If I want to do a thing I do it. Maybe I'll go to Mitya and tell him to stay with me. I did once like him, you know... for all of an hour. I think that maybe I want him again now. You see how changeable I am? What a soft-hearted, silly creature I can be.

KATERINA. I'm sure you did promise me you'd leave him alone...

GRUSHENKA. But when I think of all he's endured... and all of it for me. I think if I was to go home now, I'd feel really really sorry for Mitya. And what then?!

KATERINA *breaks a little more inside.*

Now that you understand my character I feel the need to kiss you back. Let me kiss you! I'm going to kiss you! Are you ready to be kissed?!

GRUSHENKA *holds* KATERINA *by the shoulders and is about to kiss her on the lips.*

Actually, I won't bother. Now you will always have the memory of kissing me and of not being kissed back...

KATERINA (*quick*). Slut!

GRUSHENKA. Slut?

KATERINA. Yes.

Slight pause.

GRUSHENKA. Are you talking about yourself? (*Slight pause.*) Wasn't it you who went to his hotel room and begged for money for your family? (*Whispers.*) He told me everything.

KATERINA *spits in* GRUSHENKA*'s face.*

Slight pause.

I'm going to leave you now. To stew.

GRUSHENKA *leaves.*

Scene Ten

GRUSHENKA *steps onto the dance floor and finds herself sandwiched between* FYODOR *and* MITYA. *The three dance. She slides out from between them and father and son dance face to face.*

FYODOR. Great you could come! Wouldn't have been the same without you!

MITYA. It's not every night you get to see a fat Aladdin!

51

FYODOR. I will bite your head off, chew it and spit it into the hole in your neck.

MITYA. And I'll bite yours off, chew, digest, shit it out, scoop it into an icing bag and fire it up your arsehole!

FYODOR. Complicated.

MITYA. It will be worth it.

KATERINA passes and FYODOR grabs her hand.

He suddenly has a microphone.

FYODOR. Here we are, ladies and gents! Oooooh, the happy couple! Thought this day would never come, Ivan! But now that it's here, my heart's breaking! Can you hear it? (*He makes loud crackling noises.*) Still, losing a son but gaining a daughter! Lord God, look down on this union and bless this man and his wife! Harden his resolve and soften her disposition and deliver me a little baba who calls out 'Grandpa'! (*Aside, to KATERINA.*) He did well to snatch a bride like you. You're playing down a couple of divisions! He's more dick than quick! But there is something about Mitya, I suppose! I fancy if I was a woman I'd probably take one off him! (*To the room.*) Ladies and gents, put your hands together for the groom!

He hands MITYA the microphone.

Scene Eleven

KATERINA and MITYA awkwardly dance together. Their conversation is heard over the speakers.

KATERINA. Why didn't you call me? I've been waiting all day.

MITYA. I couldn't.

KATERINA. I've something important to say relating to my relationship with you…

MITYA. I can't talk!

KATERINA. It's deeper than a love…!

MITYA. Stop! Stop it!

They stop dancing.

Pause.

KATERINA. It's only passion between you and her...

MITYA. Please, Katya!

KATERINA. What we have is deeper, Mitya!

Pause.

MITYA. You are not her. You don't add to me. You don't make me feel like she makes me feel. She is a real woman, Katya... you are the theory of a woman. She is wonderful flesh and wonderful smells... you are a flat picture to me. If I had the money I stole from you... I would repay you right now... I would end this stupid fucking engagement.

Long pause.

KATERINA *realises that she can't breathe. For some moments she searches for air as* MITYA *looks on.*

Finally she allows a long deathly breath out. She begins to breathe again.

She plays her last card.

KATERINA. But you don't have the money you stole from me?

MITYA. No.

KATERINA. Then unless you die tonight... we will still leave together. (*Slight pause.*) Now dance!

MITYA *and* KATERINA *dance.*

Scene Twelve

FYODOR *walks around, speaking into the microphone as the dance continues.*

FYODOR. In my life there's no such thing as an ugly woman. I've always been able to untap something interesting in what may outwardly be seen as an ugly bird. The very fact that she's a woman is half the story for me. Even an old woman nearing decay, flirting with dementia… even she holds a fascination for me. A handicapped woman, of soft brain, of grunts and hisses… a woman who shuffles along country roads communing with cattle and donkeys… even this simple creature I can find delight in. That's my genius, Ivan.

FYODOR *sees that* IVAN *is staring over at* KATERINA *dancing with* MITYA.

There'll be other women. Thousands of them, don't you worry about her.

IVAN (*from the depths of his soul*). I'm not… worried.

Scene Thirteen

MITYA *is in the toilet, knocking on the door.*

MITYA. It's me.

GRUSHENKA. Get out of here!

MITYA. It's the only place I can talk!

GRUSHENKA. Get out, Mitya!

MITYA (*breaking*). Please…

Long pause.

GRUSHENKA. Mitya?

Slight pause.

MITYA. I'm still here. I can't leave.

Slight pause.

GRUSHENKA. Talk to me then.

Pause.

MITYA. None of this is… simple. (*Slight pause.*) I should have worn a different costume.

He looks at the gun.

There are too many riddles in the world. So many things that need sorting. I can sometimes hear that insect scratching away inside me. (*Pause*.) All of us Karamazovs are insects... but my lust is... (*He can't find the words. Pause*.) Beauty is a terrible thing. And still I jump into the abyss, head first, heels up, and I love this degradation... it's beautiful to me. Though I'm falling with the devil, I also want to be with God. (*Pause*.) Might there be beauty in Sodom? What the mind says is shameful, the heart sees beauty and the devil fights with God and the field of battle is the human heart. I can't imagine how fat and bruised my heart must be right now. The consistency of rock probably, barely ticking over, it's a wonder how my blood travels... if it does. I think it does.

GRUSHENKA *looks over the toilet door.*

MITYA *starts singing 'Real Love' by The Beatles.*

GRUSHENKA (*interrupts him*). Hey!

MITYA *scrambles up and faces her.*

MITYA. Hi.

Pause.

If there's a reason to live, to step outside and leave this... stinking toilet, then you have to be that reason. I can't live the way I've been living. Be with me. Let's leave together tonight.

GRUSHENKA *doesn't respond. She's distant to him.*

Say something!

Pause.

GRUSHENKA. I had a dream that I was with someone... and we were on a train and it was night-time. And it was snowing outside. And on the ground the snow glistened with the moon shining on it. Like we were in Heaven. And this man held me and kissed me and it was very sweet. And we travelled far far away from here...

MITYA (*suddenly*). You will leave with me tonight, right?

Slight pause.

Grushenka?

GRUSHENKA. Let me come to you first.

MITYA. Has Fyodor given you the three thousand?

GRUSHENKA. I don't care about the money. I came here hoping
to see you...

MITYA. But he still has the money?

GRUSHENKA. I suppose he has...

MITYA. Then let me come to you later! I love you!

GRUSHENKA. You're engaged to Katerina...!

MITYA. She is a passionless sub-creature! Katerina is nothing to
you! We will leave here together tonight!

MITYA *turns and leaves.*

GRUSHENKA. Mitya...!

GRUSHENKA *comes out of the toilet and washes her hands.
She's annoyed by* MITYA*'s impatience. She looks tense,
anxious. She checks her watch. She leaves and goes to the fire
exit to wait again.*

KATERINA *appears out of the cubicle beside* GRUSHENKA*'s.
She's heard everything.*

She screams and the sound of the hand-drier is her scream.

Scene Fourteen

SMERDYAKOV *stands, listening to a troubled* ALYOSHA.

ALYOSHA. What happens to the good word? Until now, scripture
was everything to me. But scripture can't stay solely on the
page, can it?! It has to be spoken.

SMERDYAKOV. It has to be spread.

ALYOSHA. And this is what Zosima taught me!

SMERDYAKOV. Poor Zosima.

ALYOSHA. The good word exists in my heart and it forms in my
mouth. And the words take to the air. But how do they exist in
the air, Smerdyakov? How can the good word survive?

SMERDYAKOV. Is it strong enough, Alyosha?

ALYOSHA. You see, I don't think it is strong enough! And it's not a case of me shouting the good word louder so I can be heard shouting God's words above the noise. The words would then become ugly words... they would lose all their care, do you understand me?

SMERDYAKOV. I do understand.

ALYOSHA. So the words, my faith, my life leaves my mouth and takes to the world like a... like a little kitten. It leaves from the safety of the inside and out into a chaotic world, a bullying, violent world. A kitten, pure and wide-eyed, seconds from death, unloved, unwanted, an invisible kitten! This is the journey of religious faith, Smerdyakov! How can I bring myself to talk of the good word when I know it has no chance of survival in the real world?! There is no chance! It is dead, surely!

Pause.

SMERDYAKOV *watches* ALYOSHA *drinking. In an effort to reach to* ALYOSHA, *he begins:*

SMERDYAKOV. There were six kittens in that plastic bag. I placed the brick inside and made the mistake of not taking the air out of the bag as I tied it up. It was lying on the bottom of the river and the kittens had enough air for half an hour or so. I could hear their little meows as I sat on the river bank. Is it possible that one is still down there lying in the bag, breathing the last of the air? It was only three days ago, Alyosha.

ALYOSHA *recoils.*

Scene Fifteen

IVAN *stands, looking at* KATERINA *slowly crawling on the ground towards him.*

She stops and stands in front of him and tries to form a coherent apology.

KATERINA. Let me... gather. What you don't... While I don't fully understand... while I can see what I have done... There is no... never will there be a more... I don't deserve a man like... What we could have... you and me...

IVAN. Katerina Ivanovna?

KATERINA. Yes, Ivan.

IVAN. FUCK YOU!

Scene Sixteen

FYODOR, *microphone in hand, is in stand-up-comedian mode*.

FYODOR. I'll always remember how I used to creep up behind
Alyosha's mother.

MITYA *is seen loading the gun*.

I'd pay no attention to her all day long... she'd be in the kitchen
washing the dishes and I'd creep up behind her like this... I'd
throw her to the floor and reduce her to hysterics, a little tin-
kling laugh at first, a laugh of delight. Of course that delight
would precede her attacks. I'd quickly go back to the telly, turn
up the volume and then her shrieking would begin.

FYODOR *starts shrieking like his ex-wife*. MITYA *is slowly
approaching him*.

She'd be up in the bedroom... and only once I did this I swear
to God... I could hear her storming Heaven with her prayers
and crucifix. I enter the bedroom, grab her cross and yell, 'I'll
knock that mysticism right out of ya! What will happen to me if
I spit on His holy image?! Hey shrieker?!' (*He spits on the
'cross'*.) A terrible sin for which I immediately repented, but
still! How fucking funny! 'Hey shrieker?!'

IVAN. She was my mother too!

Slight pause.

FYODOR. What are you talking about?

IVAN. My mother. She was Alyosha's mother and mine!

FYODOR. Oh, right, of course she was!

FYODOR *shrieks again*.

ALYOSHA *faints, hitting his head on the table as he falls*.

The focus is on ALYOSHA *now, and* MITYA *is suddenly standing behind* FYODOR *and pointing the gun to the back of his head.*

FYODOR (*re:* ALYOSHA). Jesus fucker.

MITYA *pulls the trigger but the gun jams.*

FYODOR *turns.* MITYA *hides the gun.*

FYODOR *smiles at him.*

Scene Seventeen

FYODOR *performs 'Fools Rush In (Where Angels Fear to Tread)' by Johnny Mercer and Rube Bloom. He begins to sing it to* GRUSHENKA.

FYODOR *then sees that* GRUSHENKA *has her suitcase. She's about to leave. He runs to her.*

MITYA *appears from nowhere and floors* FYODOR *with a punch.*

MITYA *turns to* GRUSHENKA.

MITYA. What is this?! You're leaving without me?

GRUSHENKA. Yes, I'm leaving...

MITYA. But what we said! We would leave together!

GRUSHENKA. Mitya, this isn't about us!

MITYA. Of course it is! You stay here!

He takes her suitcase and throws it across the space.

GRUSHENKA. The world isn't always about you! I have someone who loves me! I'm going to him!

Pause.

You are a selfish child! People have other stories, Mitya... significant stories. You... you're lost.

She leaves without her suitcase.

MITYA *curls himself up in despair.*

Scene Eighteen

We hear a scratching noise – it is coming from inside of MITYA. *It moves from his belly into his head.*

MITYA *takes out the gun. He presses the gun against his head. He slowly presses the trigger.*

MITYA. Do it!

He can't. MITYA *lowers the gun. The scratching continues.*

It's his insect. It is him.

Horrified, MITYA *screams.*

Scene Nineteen

MITYA *walks up to* ALYOSHA *and roars.* ALYOSHA *roars back.* IVAN *joins them and the three brothers roar together.*

The brothers then enter into a delirium, tearing around the room, venting all their terrible frustrations. It's a great release.

SMERDYAKOV *tries to join in. He's briefly accepted and then forgotten about and cast aside.*

SMERDYAKOV *sees that* MITYA *has left the gun on the seat. He picks it up and places it in his pocket.*

Scene Twenty

FYODOR *opens up* GRUSHENKA'*s suitcase and rifles through her clothes.*

He finds a love letter and begins to read it.

Scene Twenty-One

IVAN *is locked in conversation with* ALYOSHA.

IVAN. ...and these stories of neighbours turning on each other, of unborn babies being cut from their mother's womb and tossed in the air and caught on bayonets. Of soldiers with little children, making them laugh and then placing a pistol inches from the child's face. The child laughs and the soldier pulls the trigger and blows its brains. We protect ourselves and say these stories are African, are racial, are not of our world... that us cultivated Europeans are a superior breed, are humane souls. But what of the five-year-old girl, in this country, whose respectable parents tortured her, who kicked and punched her until her body was one bruise! Who locked her in the basement, who smeared shit on her face, who made her insides bleed... and it was her parents who did this, Alyosha! Her parents!

SMERDYAKOV *is at the edge of the conversation.*

Her parents who slept soundly with this poor child locked in that disgusting room praying to God to protect her. If everyone must suffer to pay for eternal harmony, what have children got to do with it?! I cannot accept this?! Men and women have eaten the apple and know what good and evil is... but what do children know? They are innocents and the innocent mustn't suffer for another person's sin!

SMERDYAKOV *tries to interject, but* IVAN *pushes him away.*

And you might say that the oppressors will be avenged in hell... but what good is hell when the child has already been tortured? Why should children suffer so we can all have this promised eternal harmony? It's too high a price! It's not God that I don't accept... only I must respectfully return him the entry ticket! It's not worth the tears of that little girl locked in the basement.

SMERDYAKOV *gets too close and again* IVAN *pushes him away.*

Imagine that you are creating a fabric of human destiny with the objective of making civilisation happy, giving them eternal rest and peace at last, but that it was essential... it was inevitable to torture to death a five-year-old girl... to create this whole structure on this girl's unavenged blood and tears. Would you consent to this, Alyosha?! Could you accept this madness, tell me the truth?

ALYOSHA. No. No, I couldn't.

SMERDYAKOV. But please, Ivan...

Again, SMERDYAKOV *tries to interject.* IVAN *shoves him. He falls this time.*

IVAN (*shouts at* SMERDYAKOV). We only talked once!

Scene Twenty-Two

SMERDYAKOV *scrambles over to the mixing desk, pulls out the power cord and electrocutes himself on the chest.*

He is thrown by the shock into a frothing wreck on the floor.

The music cuts and the lights flicker.

Scene Twenty-Three

On the opposite side of the stage GRUSHENKA *is seen 'outside', lying on the ground moving slowly in a foetal position. She looks like she's in pain.*

She eventually stands. She should walk away from the club, but she turns and walks back 'inside'.

FYODOR *stands with her love letter.*

FYODOR. Didn't he turn up then? (*Slight pause.*) Does it hurt?

GRUSHENKA *turns and enters the toilet.*

Scene Twenty-Four

GRUSHENKA *and* ALYOSHA *come face to face in the toilet.*

Pause.

town. She wears a bonnet to cover her bashed head. No shoes in the snow, her feet cleansed of the memory of her father's beatings. Her ruddy face with the blank expression of idiocy lighting up her eyes like dull plastic. 'Oh, hello there!' And the people in the town look kindly on her – for surely her simplicity has her closer to God? 'If the meek will inherit the Earth surely this girl, this idiot, has God's ear?' And the town is full of open doors for her. 'Hello, special one!' A grunt, a hiss. She wanders in and out of houses. She's hanging about church, she's sleeping by the church door. There's a layer of frost on her matted hair and she's dozing in the confessional box. 'Touched by God! A special one!'

Winter to spring to summer and her bare feet stretch out on the warm ground. She's curled up sleeping in the woods when she hears the men. The gentlemen. They pull her up and there's much laughter and discussion about whether a woman like this could ever be touched. A gentleman steps forward claiming all women can be loved, 'even this creature,' he sings. His friends gone – the brandy in the man churning his insides and the idiot will be his. The idiot so often touched by God will now be touched by man.

And it's nine months since he pulled himself off her. Nine months and the people of the town name her 'whore'. Open doors are now shut doors for nine months. And where is God?! Her fat belly is dragged about town looking for the gentleman. He staggers from a bar and her baby kicks inside. She's outside the walls of his house with the rain down her face, soaking her fleece and turning her into the consistency of sponge. She can see the man inside his house, the glow of the television, the warmth from the fire, the servant at close quarters filling his glass. She's over the wall, slipping in the mud. The baby wants out! He needs to be out! He's an angry one, this one! He wants his daddy!

I'm born. The journey from muddy garden to servant at close quarters forgotten to me unlike my dead mother. An unknown, unwanted son spending his days as servant. And still those words, 'Idiot. Blockhead. Simpleton. Fathead. Thick-skulled. Shallow-of-brain. Shallow-of-thought. Spastic. Retard. Driveller-duffer-dunce. Fucking moron. Fucking imbecile. Where's my brandy?' (*Pause.*) With me, it's always doors. Standing looking at them. A shut door in my face. Standing in the kitchen looking at the door into his room. My father's room. Me the servant. The man who demanded brandy on the hour. I am stuck here. How can I retreat to the outside? For what is the outside?

The town is quiet. Little toy houses, their lights from inside blinking at each other. Little messages maybe. The moon is full and God's thrown the stars about the night sky. And isn't it so pretty what God has done? I can see my breath and it ebbs in and out like an easy music. What great harmony at this moment? How connected to the Universe I feel. What complete Oneness we have. (*Slight pause*.) And yet... I'm standing in the middle of the road and I begin to hear their cries. It's a sound that takes to the air and can be heard as far as Jupiter. A muffling yet clear cry on a crisp, clear night. Behind the closed doors you can hear them. There's a boy being dragged from his bed and placed in a box and kicked by his father until he stops crying. Another closed door and a baby being held down in a hot bath for fun maybe. Another house and a child's being raped by a stranger who's bought a ticket. Two little girls are sitting in a bedroom crying and they're the next ones for sure. And beyond this road and beyond this town and stretching out into the country and crossing oceans and spreading into more houses are the cries of many beaten children. The world fills with dark corners, of stomachs sour with salty tears. The Universe a debris of beaten bodies, of semen-covered faces. Where is God? How does He occupy Himself when there's so much suffering beneath His lovely stars? Where does He hide His conscience? Does God have a conscience? Does His heart ache a little? Does God stay in the room? Does God watch? Does He smile? Does He too want to strike the children, want to rape the girl, want to burn the boy? Where is He? (*Slight pause*.) I'm a little baby crawling in the muddy grass, away from my dead mother towards the lights of his house. There's a strength in me and with each second I'm changing from baby to boy to man. And I carry inside of me the suffering of the abandoned child. It scrapes at my insides, tears at my salty stomach and toughens my resolve! The journey from muddy garden to servant at close quarters is suddenly remembered now! It is a journey of justice! God has left this house but it is always someone's face! It is His face! His hands! His words! His needs! His abuse! Father's sin!

Without hesitation, SMERDYAKOV *takes out* MITYA*'s gun and goes to the toilet.*

He opens the door to FYODOR*'s cubicle and shoots him twice.*

He goes into the neighbouring cubicle and kills himself.

The lights go out.

Scene Twenty-Seven

In the darkness ALYOSHA *begins his impossible response.*

As he talks, the lights come up on him.

ALYOSHA. I can hear the noises on the other side of this wall. I can hear them all beneath the gunshots. And the world has buckled... and as the seconds pass it's hurrying towards what will be its end. The ground folds over itself again and again. Countries fall on other countries, continents snap and fall onto themselves. The sea mixes with the land and the sky is sucked towards all this movement, the air is squeezed into tiny pockets of unbreathable gas and the sun continues to shine on Earth as it eats itself. And the people are folded into the land and sea and animals and we're ground into paste. All our dreams, all our plans add up to nothing because it's time. The world has had enough of us. It's the end. (*Pause.*) But still, there's a word inside all this heartache. And it seems it should be lost for ever, that it could never be mined from a world wanting its end... but the word is there. And this tiny thing settles the land and places the sky above the land and the sea falls away so the animals can walk and the fish can swim. And people are standing upright again and we're looking at each other all surprised. We know that we've been saved, that 'something' has saved us. And there's a moment... before we start to talk... before we start to discuss and define who has been our saviour just now... and in that moment we look inside ourselves and see what has saved us. It's a tiny faith... an unbreakable goodness... a 'hope'. We have hope. (*Pause.*) I take it outside. I walk through the town of Mokroe with night giving way to dawn. I walk the dirt road towards the fields. All quiet, little plumes of dust kicking up from my shoes, already some warmth in the day. The road lined with flowers and tiny petals stretch out for the sun with camomile scenting the air suddenly. Away in the distance I can see the rooks shaking themselves awake and drawing black patterns in the yellow blue sky. Above the rooks and beyond the blue and the Universe continues to turn. A star fades and a child is born, the sun rises and the sun falls, the tides draw back and forth and us people breathe in and out. I push open a gate and enter a field and I walk with no great plan or purpose just lost in all this beauty. (*Slight pause.*) And I'm a child and sitting in my mother's room and watching her brush her hair in the morning time. And I'm sitting with Ivan at the kitchen table eating cherry-jam sandwiches and we're joking with Father over something or other. And maybe Mitya runs in from playing outside and Father grabs him up and tickles him, turns him upside down and my mother's leaning against the kitchen door and she's laughing… we all are. This scene plays in my heart over and over and I watch our family age. I see us bind closer to each other as the years pass with stories and dreams and the familiar. I continue walking through the fields with the past falling forward onto the future, the dream folding into a reality, the clear horizon coloured by hope and words of forgiveness and love. (*Slight pause.*) We are all alive. We can all do good. We can walk with the world with hope. (*Slight pause.*) It's always the beginning. (*Slight pause.*) So begin.

Blackout.

The End.